D0891185

Praise for *Everybody Loves Pizza*

"No matter how you slice it, everyone really does love pizza! Pollack and Ruby took on the ambitious feat of breaking it down into a delicious all-inclusive guide—and their success is proven on every page."

—Mario Batali, Food Network celebrity chef and best-selling author of four cookbooks, most recently *Molto Italiano: 327 Simple Italian Recipes To Cook at Home*

"*Everybody Loves Pizza* is a beautiful, witty, delightful guide to the history and enjoyment of nature's perfect food. You understand immediately how desperately this fabulous book was needed from the moment you read the first line of the introduction. Just try the question that Penny and Jeff asked all their friends and coworkers: 'What is your favorite pizzeria?' You'll get a different and more passionate answer from each person you ask. Which is better: Chicago's gooey deep-dish, New York's crispy slices, California's nouvelle-cuisine toppings? I share Penny and Jeff's rather promiscuous attitude about pizza: That most pizza, like most sex, is great; and even when it's bad, it's still pretty good!"

—Ted Allen, food and wine specialist on Bravo's Emmy-winning *Queer Eye* and author of the cookbook *The Food You Want to Eat*

"Immensely appetizing, tons of fun, packed with useful information including how to make it at home and where to find it everywhere in America, this book is a banquet for those of us who can never get our fill of excellent pizza."

—Jane and Michael Stern, *Gourmet* contributing editors and authors of *Roadfood*

"You're holding the single best book on pizza we've ever read. Penny Pollack and Jeff Ruby's *Everybody Loves Pizza* takes such a fun, delicious look at virtually every imaginable aspect of its subject—from its origins, to secrets of baking one, to where to find the best—that reading it is the next best thing to savoring a slice of your favorite pie. We're planning to make it our constant companion when we travel so that we'll never again miss an opportunity to taste a great pizza!"

—Andrew Dornenburg and Karen Page, James Beard Award-winning authors of *Becoming a Chef, Culinary Artistry,* and *The New American Chef*

"I can't believe two Chicago writers would take on pizza, a subject that rightfully belongs to us New Yorkers. Knowing them, I'm not surprised they succeeded. *Everybody Loves Pizza* is a terrific read."

—Alan Richman, *GQ*'s James Beard Award-winning food critic and author of *Fork It Over: The Intrepid Adventures of a Professional Eater*

NEW PORT RICHEY PUBLIC LIBRARY

AUG 1 8 2006
DISCARD

EVERYBODY LOVES
PIZZA

R. Lawrence

THE DEEP DISH ON AMERICA'S FAVORITE FOOD
by Penny Pollack and Jeff Ruby

Emmis Books  Cincinnati, Ohio

Copyright © 2005 by Penny Pollack & Jeff Ruby

All rights reserved. No portion of this book may be reproduced in any fashion, print, facsimile, or electronic, or by any method yet to be developed, without express permission of the copyright holder.

Emmis Books
1700 Madison Road, Cincinnati, Ohio 45206
www.emmisbooks.com

Edited by Jessica Yerega
Cover design by Andrea Kupper
Book interior design by Kelly N. Kofron
Front cover image courtesy of www.VintageMetalArt.com
Back cover images, from top to bottom: Courtesy of Lombardi's; courtesy of Tony Gemignani; courtesy of Arcodoro and photographer Jeff Myers

Library of Congress Cataloging-in-Publication Data
Pollack, Penny.
Everybody loves pizza : the deep dish on America's favorite food / by Penny Pollack and Jeff Ruby.
p. cm.
ISBN-13: 978-1-57860-218-6
ISBN-10: 1-57860-218-1
1. Pizza. 2. Pizza--United States. I. Ruby, Jeff. II. Title.
TX770.P58P65 2005
641.8'248--dc22
2005016714

For Steve,
who always asks whether I want an edge or a middle.
—P.P.

● ● ● ● ● ● ●

For Dad,
the only living human who doesn't love pizza.
—J.R.

ACKNOWLEDGMENTS

This book never would have happened without help from the following people:
Isaac Abella, Sarah Abella, **Bruce Allar,** Shannon Arnold, Richard Babcock, Brittney Blair,
Kelli Bozeman, Kent Brick, Steve Coomes, **Beth Dalbey,** Hillary Davis, **Kim Deeble,**
Tricia Degraff, **Annie Eichstaedt,** Will Eichstaedt, **Brandi Fisher,** Kitty Fleischman,
Nicole French, Matt Gamewell, Lynne Gantz, **Jonathan Goldsmith, Richard Gribble,**
Anne-Marie Guarnieri, Alex Hall, Andy Hall, **Barb Harris,** Joe Healy, Marilyn Heckmyer,
Jack Heffron, Amber Holst, **Bernie Hunhoff,** Laurie Hyndman, Lacey Irby, **Clive Kamins,**
Steven Keith, John Kenzie, Michelle Komie, **Kerry Ann Kraus,** Adam Kuban, **Andrea**
Kupper, Brett Kurland, Gerald Landy, Elizabeth Lenhard, **Brad Lincoln,** Walter K. Lopez,
Larry Lubliner, Beverly Magley, **Marsha Mah,** Ellen Malloy, Beth Newberry, **Jan Parr,**
Emily Perlberg, Ashley Phillips, **Adam Platt, Steve Pollack,** Robert Riethmann, Jill Rohde,
Megan Rostan, **David Ruby,** Kenn Ruby, Lois Ruby, **Debbie Sack,** Matthew Schneier,
Aviva Sinervo, Roger Sipe, Michele A. Smith, Susan Sunderland, **Kim Thornton,**
Wendy Tweedale, Steve Vest, Stefano Viglietti, **Cassie Walker, Duff Watson,** Max Weiss,
Liz Weslander, Amy Wood, **Jessica Yerega,** Andrew Zimmern, David Zivan

CONTENTS

Courtesy of Marion's

Courtesy of Bacino's; Photograph: Christopher Lowry

LAST FALL, WE ASKED EVERYONE WE KNEW one simple question: "What is your favorite pizzeria?"

We might as well have thrown a match on a can of gasoline.

The sheer volume of responses proved, if nothing else, that this book has the right title. Our friends went on to ask their friends, and so on; before we knew it, we'd received an avalanche of impassioned recommendations from coast to coast—every one of them swearing they'd found "the best pizza in the world." We got an earful from deep-dish diehards in Chicago; from brash New Yorkers who won't eat anything west of the Lincoln Tunnel; from Californians who boast their state has elevated pizza to an art form. A particularly vocal East Coast contingent claimed that any pizza not made in New Haven, Connecticut, *isn't even pizza.*

One guy in Missouri, unable to pick just one place, reeled off roughly a dozen he adored—plus the phone number of the pizzeria from his childhood. "I haven't lived in that town for twelve years," he said, "and it's the only number besides my parents' that I still know by heart." When we asked a food writer in Charleston, West Virginia, for recommendations in his state, he opened the question up to his readers—and quickly found himself inundated with contenders. Perhaps an acquaintance in New Jersey, who nominated pizzas from Boston's North End to downtown Denver, said it best: "My husband and I are pathetically obsessed with pizza."

They're not alone. Americans are fanatical about this dish, consuming approximately one hundred acres of pizza a day, or roughly 350 slices per second. But we're nothing if not opinionated, and everyone from kindergartners to classically trained chefs has a take on what makes a good pizza. Some insist that the crust is the most important element. Others say it's all about the cheese. Still another faction cries, "Forget the cheese, forget the crust; the *sauce* is the only thing that matters." The arguments go on and on.

But there's no debating one thing: Modern pizza's rise—from its humble beginnings on the streets of Naples, Italy, to become the most popular dish in the world—is no fluke. Pizza is an ideal source of protein, carbohydrates, instant nostalgia, and—

perhaps most important—it tastes damn good. "Pizza is a perfect food," *über*-foodie Jeffrey Steingarten writes in *Vogue*. "From Elizabeth David to Marcella Hazan, all gastronomes agree. It is high on my list of the hundred greatest foods on earth."

That's where this book comes in. *Everybody Loves Pizza* is a celebration of our favorite dish—its history, its versatility, its staying power. We'll tell you where it came from, where it's going, and what it means to American culture. Thanks to the help of food writers, pizza insiders, and ordinary, pizza-loving Americans, we'll also tell you where to find 546 top-notch pizzerias across the country. And, with our definitive list of the ten best pizzas in America, we plan to start some arguments of our own.

Along the way, we pay homage to the muscle-bound guy behind the counter in the T-shirt flipping and stretching his dough, the pepperoni-faced competitive eater testing the limits of his stomach, the cerebral pizzaiolo dedicated to the delicate art of the pie—and every other pathetically obsessed subculture that has popped up around this most iconic dish.

Chicago pizza pioneers Rudy Malnati and Ike Sewell, along with Florence Sewell and another guest at Malnati's wedding

Courtesy of Lou Malnati's Pizzeria

Courtesy of Lombardi's

CHAPTER 1
History of the Pizza World

Courtesy of Metro Pizza

ASK ONE HUNDRED FOOD HISTORIANS about the origins of pizza and you're likely to get one hundred different answers. Separating the fact from the fiction is no easy task. This much is certain: It all starts with crust.

Pizza's history is intertwined with the history of bread, which means the first proto-pizzas probably were eaten sometime between the twelfth and third millennia B.C. in the southeast Mediterranean region. We're not talking sixteen-inch deep-dish pepperoni here, but rather a crude bread that was baked beneath the stones of a fire. The bread was seasoned with a variety of primitive toppings and probably was used to sop up broth or gravy. Ed LaDou, the legendary California pizza maker, has always said that pizza, at its heart, is essentially an edible plate—sturdy enough to take with you and eat anywhere.

Many say the idea of using bread as a plate came from the Greeks, who ate flat round bread called *plankuntos* baked with an assortment of indigenous toppings. Ancient Egyptians reportedly had a custom of celebrating the Pharaoh's birthday with a seasoned flat bread. Other texts suggest the Romans or the Phoenicians were first. Most likely it was all four cultures—and countless others—who figured out that mixing flour with water, heating it on hot stones, and putting stuff on it was a pretty good idea.

At the height of the Persian Empire, the soldiers of Darius the Great (521–486 B.C.) reportedly baked bread flat upon their shields and then covered it with cheese and dates during long marches. Not long after, Cato the Elder (234–149 B.C.), in his written history of Rome, described a "flat round of dough dressed with olive oil, herbs, and honey baked on stones." Marcus Gavius Apicius (b. 25 B.C.), Rome's original foodie, wrote a legendary cookbook called *De Re Coquinaria* featuring recipes with a hollowed-out loaf of bread topped with cheese, garlic, chicken, mint, pepper, and oil. (We love the touch of mint: dinner and breath freshener in one.)

Above: Turn-of-the-century pizza equipment; opposite: Gennaro Lombardi, who opened America's first pizzeria in 1905

A two-thousand-year-old oven in the ruins of Pompeii

In 79 A.D., Mount Vesuvius, a volcano along the Bay of Naples, erupted. Volcanic ash and dust spewed across Pompeii until the entire town of twenty thousand people was buried. Those who didn't die ran for their lives. The event essentially wiped Pompeii from the map until it eventually became just an expanse of grass and vines; for more than 1,500 years, it sat dormant. In the 1800s, archaeologists excavated the area, and what they found was astounding: temples and businesses; streets; a brothel; families frozen in time, huddling together at their last moment. And they found hints not only that a flat flour cake was widely eaten in Neopolis (a Greek colony that became Naples), but also that there were shops—decked with marble slabs and other tools of the trade—that looked an awful lot like today's pizzerias.

There are also several theories about the origin of the word "pizza." The most likely is that it came from an Old Italian word meaning "a point," which evolved into the Italian word "pizziare" (roughly, "to pinch" or "pluck"). According to John Mariani's *The Dictionary of Italian Food and Drink*, the word first surfaced around 1000 A.D. as "picea" or "piza," most likely as a reference to the way the cook had to yank the hot pie from the oven. Around the same time, some of the world's more skilled cooks were refining and perfecting focaccias, topping them with anchovies, mushrooms, and whatever else they could get their hands on. Apparently great minds think alike.

> "Without question, the greatest invention in the history of mankind is beer. Oh, I grant you that the wheel was also a fine invention, but the wheel does not go nearly as well with pizza."
> —humorist Dave Barry

FAST FORWARD to 1522.

That year, one seemingly small event changed the landscape of food forever, putting all the tools in place for pizza's improbable ascension: Spanish explorers brought back tomatoes from the Andes of Peru. The rest of Europe turned up its collective nose, assuming these strange new fruits were poisonous. Most avoided tomatoes for centuries. But the lower classes in Naples—which lived on flour, olive oil, lard, cheese, and herbs—began adding the city's crop of particularly sweet tomatoes to the mix. According to Professor Carlo Mangoni, who teaches nutrition at the Second University of Naples, tomato and bread joined forces in roughly 1760, and the modern pizza was born.

"In various parts of Europe as late as the end of the eighteenth century," writes Rosario Buonassisi in *Pizza* (Firefly, 2000), "when salt was still a luxury, the poorer classes used to salt their foods with a mixture of salt and ashes from a wood fire, or when poverty was extreme, with ashes alone." In other words, pizza was a dish born of scarcity. It was so lowly a street food that there is little documentation about its early days because anyone who was making and eating it was most likely illiterate—and definitely not bragging about his modest diet.

By the early nineteenth century, Neapolitans were buying and selling pizza on the street for breakfast, lunch, and dinner. Eventually, someone got the bright idea of setting up a stall and making the dough while customers ordered—and watched. "Pizzerias," boisterous, open-air gathering places, began to pop up all over the area. The earliest of record was Antica Pizzeria Port'Alba—which opened in 1830 and to this day still makes pizzas in a wood-fired oven lined with lava rocks from the nearby Mount Vesuvius.

Deep-fried pizza is so popular in **SCOTLAND** that you can buy it in most fish-and-chip shops there.

MOST POPULAR TOPPINGS AROUND THE WORLD

AUSTRALIA
ham and pineapple

INDIA
pickled ginger, mutton, and tofu

RUSSIA
red herring

BRAZIL
green peas

JAPAN
sweet corn; squid

UNITED STATES
pepperoni

COSTA RICA
coconut

PAKISTAN
curry

EUROPE
tuna

At some point, a pizzaiolo (Italian for "pizza maker"), whose name is lost in the annals of history, decided to make a pizza with the same kind of tomato sauce that Italians loved with their pasta. He spread a thinner version of the pasta sauce on his pizzas, and no matter how hot his oven got, the tomatoes kept the flatbread soft, pliable, and moist. His innovation caught on immediately, and pizza chefs everywhere, thrilled with the popularity of the new version, ran with it. The pizzas that Neapolitans cooked were simple—ten inches of flatbread with a crispy, charred rim, fresh tomatoes grown in the rich volcanic ash of Vesuvius, mozzarella cheese (from cow's or buffalo's milk), a little olive oil, and maybe a couple of basil leaves or some garlic.

Eventually curious members of Italy's upper crust began to journey into the slums of Naples to try this "new" dish they'd heard so much about. They were not disappointed. The Queen of Naples, Maria Carolina d'Asburgo Lorena (1752–1814), grew so fond of pizza that she commissioned a custom oven to be built in the royal summer palace. By the mid-eighteenth century, tomatoes replaced garlic and lard as the favored pizza topping, and "red" pizzas entered the mainstream with such a force that they were the most common food in Naples and the surrounding areas.

ONE PIZZERIA, called Pietro il Pizzaiolo (later renamed Pizzeria Brandi), quickly set itself apart from the competition. Its owner and talented pizzaiolo, Raffaele Esposito, was considered the best in town, and he was justifiably proud of his mastery of the oven. He was talented, but, like so many others who make it into the history books, he also happened to be in the right place at the right time.

On June, 11, 1889, the king of Italy, Umberto I (1844–1900), and his wife, Queen Margherita di Savoia (1851–1926)—who had once resided in Naples—found themselves back in town for a vacation. The queen recently had been causing waves by eating this "lower-class" dish amongst her subjects: unseemly behavior for royalty. When they arrived in Naples, the queen, who had heard that Esposito was the best, requested that he visit the Naples palazzo and make some of these Neapolitan "pizzas." It was essentially the first pizza delivery.

Esposito, flattered, prepared one of the most famous dinners in the history of food. He served three varieties of pizza: One had pork fat, cheese, and basil; another had tomatoes, garlic, and olive oil; a third had tomatoes, mozzarella, and basil. The queen was delighted with her meal.

PATRIOT ACT

One popular myth says that Raffaele Esposito's wife, Pasqualina Brandi, threw a few leaves of basil on her husband's famous pizza so that it would match the colors of the Italian flag and earn the favor of the queen. It's far more likely that Neapolitan pizzaioli had been throwing basil on pizzas for years, but hey, it makes a nice story.

DRUMROLL, PLEASE

The early pizza seller in Naples was typically a boy paid to walk the streets carrying a copper cylindrical drum full of pizzas on his head. The drum advertised the name of the pizzeria and had a false bottom that was packed with charcoal from the oven to keep the pizzas hot. A century later, when pizza was introduced to Chicago on Taylor Street—the Windy City's Little Italy—it was in much the same way.

left: © 2005 Wisconsin Milk Marketing Board, Inc.; right photograph: Jonathan Goldsmith

Left: Fresh Wisconsin mozzarella cheese, used on many American pizzas today; above: traditional pizza fresh from the oven in Italy

In fact, she so adored the tomato-mozzarella-basil pizza that she sent Esposito a letter of praise. Overjoyed, the pizzaiolo named the version after her, and a legend—the pizza Margherita, the standard for all pizzas since—was born.

Word spread, and it wasn't long before Naples was the pizza capital of the world, a title it still proudly claims. "Send an American to Naples and it is as if he or she has seen the burning bush," Peter Reinhart wrote more than one hundred years later in *American Pie.* "That person's pizza world has been rocked and will never be the same again, or so it seems." ● ● ●

Chicago

New York

New Haven

California

Photograph: Gerald Landy (New Haven); Courtesy of Lombardi's (New York); Courtesy of Pizzeria Uno (Chicago); Photograph: Jonathan Goldsmith (California)

CHAPTER 2
The United States of Pizza

Courtesy of 3 Tomatoes & a Mozzarella

AMERICAN PIZZAS ARE LIKE SNOWFLAKES: No two are exactly alike. There are endless regional pizza variations in this country, and everyone's got a favorite. We're not masochistic enough to enter the debate as to which style is best: We're here to celebrate them all. But we have singled out the four areas with the richest pizza histories and lore—New York, New Haven, Chicago, and California—and delved a little deeper into the origins of their famous pies.

What we learned is that while pizza may not have been born in the States, that's definitely where it grew up. And though it's been around for centuries, pizza has adapted and evolved more in the past one hundred years than any food ever has. It has gone from a thin pie made with simple ingredients, to a massive, complicated double-crusted beast, to a pliable vessel for every topping under the sun—and back to a thin pie with simple ingredients. "I am certain that were it not for the American embrace of pizza," master pizza maker Ed LaDou writes on his Web site, "the Italian pizzeria would be as common today as it was forty or fifty years ago: barely recognized."

New York

"When they got to America, they learned three things: that the streets were not paved with gold; that the streets were not paved at all; and that they were expected to pave them." —Italian inscription at Ellis Island museum

ITALIAN IMMIGRANTS BEGAN TO LAND on New York's shores in 1872, and soon they came in droves. The first wave was predominantly Northern Italian. But eventually, most who arrived were peasants who hailed from Southern Italy—a land they loved with all their heart, but a land they'd felt compelled to leave in search of the usual things: health, prosperity, *a better life.*

In contrast to Southern Italy's brutal poverty and unemployment, America, they found, could put unskilled laborers and artisans to work. By 1920, more than seven million Italians were living in the United States, establishing their own inner-city "Little Italies"—on the Lower East Side of Manhattan, in Boston's North End, in South Philadelphia, in Chicago's Near West Side. They brought with them their many dialects, their music, their ingenuity—and their food.

New York got the bulk of the Italian influx. In 1904 alone, 575,000 Italians reached New York City through Ellis Island, and they created a close-knit (if uncomfortable) community that centered on Mulberry Street. Many of them shopped at a grocery in the heart of the neighborhood at 53½ Spring Street. The store, which opened in 1897, was run by a native of Naples, an ordinary baker named Gennaro Lombardi. It was a small, cramped place outfitted with a coal-fired brick oven that Lombardi used for baking bread from a recipe his ancestors had cherished and passed down in the old country.

The Lombardi family in its pizzeria

Photos both pages courtesy of Lombardi's

Soon, to use up the excess dough each day, he began imitating the cheese pies that had recently taken Naples by storm. In Italy, pizzas were made in a wood-burning oven, but the most economic fuel in New York was coal, which was fine with Lombardi. His coal oven generated intense heat, and though the pizzas he produced weren't exactly Neapolitan, they were equally distinctive—soft, crisp crust; smoky, lightly charred bottom; tomato and cheese sticking to the bread. Lombardi wrapped the pizzas in paper, tied them with string, and sold them to Italian blue-collar workers looking for something easy to take for lunch. He sold large pizzas for fifteen cents.

Gennaro Lombardi may not have been the first; documents suggest that Neapolitan bakers in New York had been serving pizza as early as 1895. He may not necessarily have been the best, either. But he was the most successful, and in 1905—seventy-five years after the first pizzeria in Naples opened—Lombardi's Pizzeria was granted America's first mercantile license to bake pizza.

Lombardi's original storefront

ONE OF LOMBARDI'S FRIENDS from Naples, Anthony "Totonno" Pero, was only seventeen when he arrived in New York in 1905, but he already knew his way around an oven. Ever ambitious, Pero asked his old friend to let him make pizzas in the coal oven on Spring Street. Lombardi relented, and Pero became Lombardi's pizzaiolo.

Right: Anthony "Totonno" Pero; below: Jerry Pero, Totonno's son

For the next two decades, he crafted some of New York's most legendary pizzas.

By 1924, Pero had saved enough to go into business for himself, and he left Lombardi's to open Totonno's Pizzeria fourteen miles away in Coney Island. Pero, who, of course, installed his own coal-fired oven at his own place, became the quintessential New York pizzaiolo. "Back then, Anthony only made so much dough for the day," Larry Goldberg, Totonno's current co-owner, told *Pizza Marketing Quarterly* in 2003. "When it was gone, that was it." If a customer didn't like the looks of his pizza and found reason to complain, Pero— who had no shortage of patrons—took back the pizza and told them to beat it.

In 1929, another Lombardi's protégé, John Sasso, left to open the seminal John's Pizzeria in the heart of Greenwich Village. Sasso, who sold only whole pizzas in the Neapolitan tradition, put a proud sign in the window that showed he was all business: "No Slices." At the time, pizza was still an obscure ethnic food, but Sasso must have noticed the new pizzerias and cafes popping up around New York, many of which were cutting their pizzas into smaller servings. Old school to the end, Sasso foresaw—and lamented—the coming of a New York trend that would take pizza further away from its Italian roots: the slice.

Perhaps the most renowned slice purveyor in Manhattan was—and still is—Patsy's, which opened in 1933 in an unassuming East Harlem storefront. Little more than a counter, a coal-fired brick oven, and a plain dining room, Patsy's was one of the first to take traditional New York pizza and make it

Both photos courtesy of Totonno's

available fast, cheap, and in single wedges. This may have amounted to blasphemy to old-timers like Sasso, but it was pure gold for owner Pasquale "Patsy" Lancieri. And if anyone could get away with it, it was Lancieri—himself another reported Lombardi's disciple.

But it wasn't until U.S. soldiers returned home from World War II—where many of them had served on the Italian front—that pizza made its jump into the American mainstream. "I remember the first time I tried it, I had no idea what the heck it was," says George Saxe, an Army veteran who now lives in the San Francisco area. "But I loved the stuff—just not the droopy kind." As veterans searched for pizza in their home country, pizza began to break out of its Italian enclaves. And, as always, technology adapted to the new demand. The emergence of high-speed commercial mixers and cheaper gas-fired ovens meant that pizza makers could produce quick, hot slices, which led to a higher-volume business.

The slice, it turned out, was a perfect fit for New Yorkers, who were always on the go. It became a tradition to showcase pizzas in a front window so that passersby—who didn't even realize they were hungry—would see and smell the pizza, grab a slice for mere pocket change, and eat it on a paper plate while walking down the street. People coming the other way would see the lucky pizza eater and inexplicably find themselves drawn to the source. Madison Avenue has yet to produce a more effective ad campaign.

JOHN'S PIZZERIA
At John's Pizzeria (New York, New York) the oven is older than the parlor (the place was a bakery first).

Photograph: Larry Lubliner

TODAY YOU CAN'T WALK a block in Manhattan without passing a pizzeria: Most estimates put the number at more than three thousand in the New York area. Ask a resident which one is the best and you're likely to get an earful; locals defend their favorites with a loyalty that borders on scary. They're famously educated on pizza's history and can trace the New York City family tree for you—with Lombardi's at the root. Many of them will insist that John's on Bleecker Street (which, after seventy-five years, still has the "no slices" sign in the window) surpassed Lombardi's years ago. Totonno's is equally beloved in Coney Island; others swear by DiFara Pizza or Grimaldi's in Brooklyn, or Nick's in Queens.

In fact, even the granddaddy of them all fell on hard times. When Gennaro Lombardi died, his son John took over, the clientele and neighborhood changed, and, in 1984, after seventy-nine years in business, Lombardi's closed.

But ten years later, Gennaro's grandson, Jerry—along with childhood buddy John Brescio—reopened Lombardi's in a century-old building a block away at 33 Spring Street. The new locale even has its own coal-fired oven. Like the old oven, it reaches nine hundred degrees, fits about seven pizzas at a time, and bakes each of them in roughly three and a half minutes. (Because of environmental concerns, new coal ovens have been outlawed in New York, but Lombardi's and a few others were grandfathered in.) It was a brilliant move. Pizza fanatics from all over the world now make the pilgrimage to Spring Street to taste a little coal-fired history, and at the ripe old age of one hundred, Lombardi's—all brick, stucco, and vintage photographs—is New York's most famous pizzeria.

It was also a heart-warming move, one that solidified Gennaro Lombardi's place as America's "Patriaca dela Pizza": the Father of American Pizza.

> The pizza that John Travolta famously folded at the beginning of *Saturday Night Fever* came from **LENNY'S PIZZA** (Brooklyn, New York).

DOMENICO DE MARCO

12 REASONS WHY DOMENICO DE MARCO, 70, OF DIFARA PIZZA IN BROOKLYN, IS THE QUINTESSENTIAL OLD SCHOOL AMERICAN PIZZAIOLO:

① He arrives at 7:00 every morning to fire up the oven.

② He handcrafts every pizza himself.

③ He makes 1 dough ball at a time, and grates only enough cheese for 1 pizza.

④ He grows fresh herbs in his window box.

⑤ He hasn't taken a day off since 1989—when he went to Italy.

⑥ He puts the pizza in the oven on a paddle, but pulls it out with his hands so he can squeeze the collar.

⑦ The most pizzas he can fit in his oven at one time is 3.

⑧ After he takes the pizza out of the oven, he "waits until his inner voice" tells him to cut the pizza.

⑨ He refuses to allow his son to make pizzas. He hasn't even shown him how.

⑩ When he closes at the end of the day, he has a slice of pizza and a $100

bottle of Amarone Valpolicella—he buys 1 bottle a day and 2 on Saturday because the liquor store is closed on Sunday.

⑪ He doesn't get home until around 2:00 in the morning.

⑫ He's back at 7:00 the next morning to fire up the oven.

Photograph: Larry Lubliner

Photograph: Michelle Komie

**Lou Abate, owner
of Abate Apizza
in New Haven,
with a pepperoni pie**

New Haven

·······················

IN FORTY-NINE STATES, New York City is generally considered the
uncontested birthplace of U.S. pizza. The lone dissenter is Connecticut. Whether
or not today's descendants of New Haven's early Italian pioneers acknowledge
New York as a claimant, there's no denying this small college town seventy miles
north of the Big Apple has a pizza history every bit as rich—and contentious—as
Manhattan's legacy.

    In 1870, New Haven's entire Italian-born population numbered ten. For the same
reasons that Northern Italians found their way to New York—overcrowding and poor
conditions back home—immigrants from Southern Italian towns such as Amalfi began
to flood Connecticut by the turn of the century. As early as 1910, more than thirteen
thousand Italians lived in New Haven, most of them in an area called Wooster Square.
They settled there because no one else wanted to. A formerly wealthy neighborhood ten
miles from Yale University, by the late nineteenth century Wooster Square had devolved
into gritty rows of tenements and factories. Before long the area was dubbed "Little
Naples" and had become New Haven's most thriving ethnic neighborhood, crammed
with Italian mechanics, painters, banks, and shoemakers. The streets teemed with
pushcarts full of homemade sausages and kids playing baseball in vacant lots.

Frank Pepe displays one of his famous New Haven pies

Courtesy of Frank Pepe Pizzeria Napoletana

One of the neighborhood's familiar faces was a Maiori native named Frank Pepe. The quintessential Wooster Square Italian immigrant (poor, uneducated, enthusiastic), Pepe took a job at a New Haven factory, but he hated it. He had done some baking back in Maiori, and soon he landed a job at a bakery at 163 Wooster Street, which proved to be a much better fit for him. One day, for whatever reason, he flattened some dough and threw on some goodies—perhaps olive oil, oregano, and anchovies. Whether he was influenced by the New Yorkers (not likely), the Neapolitans (perhaps), or his own ingenuity (the best bet), he slid it into the bakery's coal-fired oven.

What came out was history. Pepe started to cart variations of his pies up and down the street in a wagon and sell them for twenty-five cents, and according to Elissa Altman of the *Hartford Courant,* his creation became so popular that he began to "out[sell] his employer before buying the business right out from under him." He remodeled the tiny space at 163 Wooster and, in June 1925, opened Frank Pepe Pizzeria Napoletana.

A small but fierce coterie of customers made the place their hangout, drawn to the fresh pies—and to the colorful personality of Pepe himself, who reportedly used to smack unruly customers with his long wooden pizza peel. Although the place was a hit with Wooster Square locals, it took some time for non-Italians to notice; most of them didn't know what pizza was, and they couldn't even pronounce the name of the dish to Pepe's satisfaction. (He called it "apizza" [ah-BEETS], using the old Sicilian slang.)

Ironically, Pepe was allergic to tomatoes *and* mozzarella, but it was these limitations that led to his most famous creation. In addition to simple pizzas, the restaurant served littleneck clams on the half shell; it was only a matter of time before the clams made their way onto the pies. The result, an irregularly shaped "white clam pie," was unlike anything anyone had seen: whole freshly shucked clams with garlic, oregano, and olive oil on a crisp thin cornmeal-dusted crust that proved extraordinarily supple because it wasn't saddled with mozzarella and tomato sauce. Where New York pizza was deliciously flaccid, Pepe's coal-oven version stood up at attention like the pizzas from the old country.

Frank Pepe had created an instant American classic that evolved into one of the most universally hallowed food creations in the country—and he managed to do it while allergic to pizza's basic components. It was the pizza world's equivalent to Beethoven composing his Ninth Symphony while deaf.

AS PEPE'S LEGEND GREW, so did New Haven's demand for pizza. In 1934, soon-to-be rival Modern Apizza opened a mile away with similar but thicker pies that were embraced by locals from the beginning. But there was enough demand to support more than one pizza parlor, and even as the neighborhood deteriorated, Frank Pepe's continued to boom. He got his family involved, and in 1936, to accommodate the non-stop lines that spilled out onto Wooster Street, he moved into a bigger space next door.

Around the same time, Pepe's nephews Salvatore ("Sally") and Tony Consiglio, who had been working at the parlor since they were teenagers, left. (Rumors still swirl that it was against their uncle's wishes.) The Consiglios were young and ambitious, and they had learned the art of pizza from a true master. With their mother, the brothers opened their own coal-oven pizzeria just down the street at 238 Wooster. "My mother wanted to call the restaurant Sally's and Tony's," Tony Consiglio, now eighty-seven, told *Yankee* magazine in 2000. "To have a beer permit, you had to be twenty-one. My brother was twenty-one. I was nineteen." And so, in 1938, it opened (with a beer permit) as Sally's Apizza. The same year, the city designated Little Naples a "blighted area."

Sally's was smaller and darker than Pepe's—and its servers notoriously grumpy—but Sally had learned well: The pies were as miraculous as his mentor's up the street. Like Pepe's, they were oblong, but thinner, spicier, and known for perfectly cooked mozzarella (pronounced "mootz" in New Haven). Sally's most famous devotee was Frank Sinatra, who used to send a driver to New Haven to bring back pies when he was performing in New York. "I think it helped his voice," Tony Consiglio said. Like Pepe's, these pizzas were good enough to trigger long lines out front, lines that built up the delicious anticipation—and made everyone seem like an old friend by the time you got inside.

"THERE WAS NO FEUD," says Francis Rosselli, a grandson of Frank Pepe and partner at Pepe's pizzeria. "That has become a myth, fabricated by the fact that Sally's had its own contingency of clientele." The long rivalry between Sally's and Pepe's—whether real or imagined—is very real among their patrons. For generations, New Havenites have pledged undying loyalty to one pizzeria and lifelong loathing for the other; it's not uncommon for arguments about which is better to end in bloodshed. Others argue over whether or not there's a rivalry at all."

At Pepe's, those with a view of the famous twelve-foot-by-twelve-foot oven endure uncomfortable wooden booths so they can witness the daily creation of pure pizza magic. Many grumble that they wouldn't be caught dead at Sally's. At Sally's, when regulars mysteriously manage to circumvent the line, those they've jumped in front of simply shrug. It's all part of the history—and it's worth it. "There are only two things in life you stand in line for," Tom Dudchik, a former state legislator, told the *New York Times* in 1989. "Communion and Sally's pizza."

SKIPPER'S (Madison, South Dakota) has a pizza called "Hooligans" named for 2 patrons who worked for free to pay down their bar bill.

Chris Rioux, owner of **CHRIS-TOPHER PIZZA CO.** (Nashville, Tennessee), on his pizzeria's hours of operation: "We open when we're ready and close when we're tired."

The area around Wooster Street, after decades of struggle and eventual renewal, has become a historic district. Its streets are lined with lovely townhouses and cherry trees. It certainly doesn't look like the site of a holy war—or the birthplace of an American art form. Yet swarms of tourists wander up and down Wooster to decide for themselves, endlessly debating the merits of Pepe's crust or Sally's cheese. (Or the similar pies from the Pepe's-owned alternative, The Spot, which is in the original Pepe's space.) Whatever they pick, most come away agreeing on one thing: Wooster Street is the epicenter of America's controversial pizza history.

Frank and Sally are both long gone, but the lines outside their pizzerias remain. And the bad blood between the branches of the family—if it ever existed to begin with—is gone. Gary Bimonte, another Pepe grandson, says the cold war is history, and Bob Consiglio, co-owner of Sally's, agrees. But if you press Bimonte, he admits that he has never been to Sally's; Consiglio, who is Frank Pepe's brother's daughter's son, has never eaten at Pepe's. And he doesn't intend to go any time soon.

TONY CONSIGLIO
AN ORIGINAL PARTNER AT SALLY'S APIZZA REMINISCES ABOUT THE GOOD OLD DAYS:

There were only 2 kinds of pizza in those days. Grated cheese and tomatoes—that was a plain pizza—and the other one had anchovies, tomatoes, oregano, and olive oil. And that was it. One day, Sam Jacobs, who had a produce market on State Street in New Haven, came in with an onion. He said to my mother, "Cut this onion up and put it on the pizza for me. With the tomatoes." People started to come in and ask for onion pies, so we had to make them, too.

In those days there was no competition. When we started the pizza business in 1938, a small was 25¢ and a medium was 50¢. A small was 8 inches, a medium was 12 inches. Sally, my older brother, he ran the show. My sisters, Connie and Sara, were the waitresses. In the kitchen, Sally and me, and my other brother—may he rest in peace—Andy. My mother, Filomena, made sure the money went in the cash register. Frank Pepe and my mother were brother and sister.

I worked as Frank Sinatra's personal assistant for 30 years, got his clothes ready. He came in with the Tommy Dorsey Band. And then followed Louis Prima. Johnny Mathis. Lou Gehrig. Muhammad Ali. The Kennedys. Martin and Lewis. Abbott and Costello, who weren't talking to each other—so the pictures were taken separately. Sal passed away and his wife and children are running Sally's now. I'm too old to be there, but I still keep in touch.

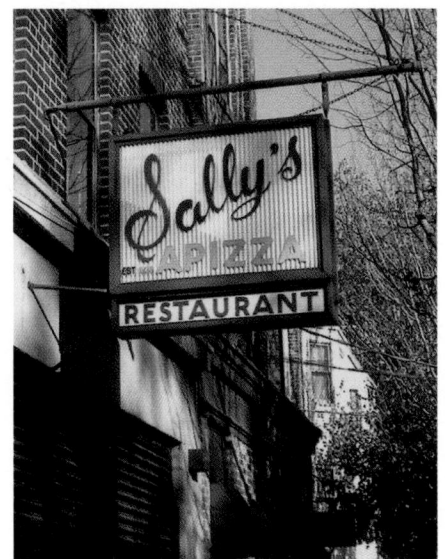

Photograph: Steve Pollack

Chicago

IN CHICAGO, no one cares whether American pizza was invented in New York or New Haven or New Zealand. Chicagoans are interested only in where it was perfected: on the western shores of Lake Michigan, of course. The two thousand or so pizzerias lining Chicago's streets—many devoted to their own versions of a hearty local innovation—attest to the Windy City's love of pizza. The city's strong Italian legacy in the twentieth century is well documented (for better or worse), but deep-dish pizza will always be its most famous Italian export, and it remains perhaps the most loved and loathed pizza spin in the world.

Ike Sewell, co-founder of Pizzeria Uno

The only thing thicker than the deep-dish pizzas in Chicago are the legends surrounding their genesis. History, perhaps unfairly, has given credit to Ike Sewell, a backslapping former all-American football player at the University of Texas. In the early 1940s, Sewell, then an executive with a distillery company, noticed there were no decent *Mexican* restaurants in Chicago, and approached Ric Riccardo Sr., a flamboyant Chicago restaurateur, to go into business. The two took out a lease on the basement of an old mansion on the corner of Ohio and Wabash on Chicago's Near North Side and began painting bullfight murals on the walls.

The trouble was, Riccardo, who was of Italian descent, had never tried Mexican food. He didn't even know what it tasted like, so how could he possibly serve it? Sewell always maintained that a Mexican bartender at Riccardo's tavern on Rush Street—who claimed to have learned a thing or two from his mother in the kitchen—fixed them a meal. Thank God the guy was a lousy cook. The menu of his infamous meal (along with his name) went unrecorded, but whatever it was, it made Riccardo violently ill. "He always said it was the worst meal he ever had in his life," Sewell said later.

What happened next is unclear. Everyone seems to agree that Riccardo disappeared to Italy for a couple of months, but no one knows why he went. Some say that he went to visit his sick mother; other accounts report that he fought in World War II. Sewell claimed Riccardo just grabbed all his (Riccardo's) money and took off. Regardless of why he left, when he returned he was armed with a better idea: Why not open a pizzeria?

Courtesy of Pizzeria Uno

He made a traditional pizza for Sewell, who was skeptical; this thin, delicate appetizer was too frail for a big Texan like him. Besides, you could already get the stuff in Little Italy across town. According to Sewell, the two returned to the kitchen and began experimenting. They came up with a brawnier, knife-and-fork version of pizza that both could live with, a version more befitting of Chicago's Big-Shouldered history. It was a beast of a meal—thick, flaky crust more than an inch tall, an insane amount of cheese and toppings, a dense layer of sauce on top rather than underneath. In fact, the entire pizza was assembled in reverse order: Mozzarella was placed directly on the dough; toppings were spread on the cheese, then came whole chunks of plum tomatoes; then a little bit more cheese. Sewell and Riccardo had deep-dish pans specially made just for their pizzas. The newly energized partners painted over the bullfight mural and opened on December 6, 1943.

When Riccardo and Sewell unveiled Pizzeria Uno—a dark, tiny place with low ceilings and a weird spin on an already obscure dish—Chicagoans barely noticed. Those who did were confused: Even the few who had heard of pizza said this wasn't it. The fact that the pies took thirty to forty-five minutes to bake didn't help matters. Sewell, ever the salesman, started giving it away for free at the bar and telling strangers on the street to come in, but business was still lousy.

Just when it looked like Uno was going to tank, a reporter who had served in Italy during the war discovered the place. (No one can remember the fellow's name.) He wrote an article boasting that this heavy pie was better than any pizza he'd had abroad. That got Chicago's attention. Slowly the dish went from an oddity to a favorite to a legend, and crowds jammed the place from open to close. There were so many people clamoring for deep-dish pizza that in 1955 Sewell opened Pizzeria Due a block away in an old Victorian house and used the same secret recipe. It was also a huge success.

Soon, more than just Chicagoans were eating deep-dish. It became a tradition among Midwesterners passing through to stop in at Uno or Due. The pizza was so filling, most could only eat one or two pieces, and the rest would go home in doggy bags.

Courtesy of Pizzeria Uno

Courtesy of Pizzeria Uno

Frank Sinatra, obviously not a regional partisan when it came to pizza, had Uno delivered to his room at the Ambassador East when he was in town. (No word on whether it helped his voice.) But many East Coasters rolled their eyes, calling deep-dish a casserole, a travesty, or worse. Even within Chicago, it had its detractors. Mike Royko, the famous newspaper columnist, made his displeasure known in his column: "If you try to pick up a piece of deep-dish pizza, you might get a hernia. Or it could fall on your lap and break your thigh bone."

Sewell continually vowed he would never franchise his operation. "When you get too big, the quality goes down proportionally," he said in 1977. He reportedly received 2,500 offers from business-men over the years, and he turned them all down—until a Kentucky Fried Chicken bigwig named Aaron Spencer finally got to him. Spencer convinced Sewell that people were ripping off his creation all over the country and he wasn't getting a cent. When Sewell signed the papers in 1979 and the company head-quarters moved to Boston, it broke the hearts of countless Chicagoans—who declared it the end of an era.

But it thrilled considerably more people across the nation. Today there are more than two hundred Uno Chicago Grills in the United States (and as far away as South Korea), and the menu has expanded to include such crowd-pleasing items as fish and chips and nachos. Chicagoans, naturally, wouldn't be caught dead in any of them, other than the original and its brother up the street. Spencer, the CEO of the highly successful Uno Restaurant Holdings Corporation, insists the original pizza formula hasn't changed.

Above: Pizzera Uno's deep-dish—a Chicago classic; opposite: Ike Sewell and Aaron Spencer; the original Pizzeria Uno

LIKE LOMBARDI'S in New York and Pepe's in New Haven, Pizzeria Uno is at the root of a complicated family tree. Countless Uno alumni defected to establish their own restaurants. Alice Mae Redmond, Uno's soft-spoken pizza chef, was perhaps the most popular. Redmond left in the sixties with her "secret dough conditioner" and joined forces with an unlikely trio—a pair of local cab drivers and a Sicilian butcher—who had recently purchased a building just east of Michigan Avenue. They wanted to serve deep-dish pizza, but had no idea how to do it. Enter Redmond. She recruited her sister, Ruth Hudley, and the two of them developed a secret recipe based on Redmond's time at Uno.

THE DISH DEEPENS

Ike Sewell, whose name is now synonymous with Chicago-style pizza, repeated colorful stories about Uno's good old days until 1990, when he died a very wealthy man. But what of Ric Riccardo Sr.? He passed away in 1954, the year before Due opened, and his name is often no more than a footnote in Chicago's pizza history. In 1993, Mike Royko went to bat for him in his *Chicago Tribune* column: "The fact is, Ike Sewell knew a couple of Chicago Italians named Rudy Malnati and Ric Riccardo Sr. . . . They came up with the deep-dish concept, and Ike Sewell marketed it."

Mae Juel Allen, Riccardo's ex-wife, lashed out at the Sewell saga in a 1999 article in *Chicago* magazine, in which she argued that Riccardo launched the pizzeria himself and Sewell didn't come along until a year after the place opened. "Ike Sewell didn't know beans about deep-dish pizza," Allen said. "I think Sewell was a crook." An early Uno patron named Marilew Kogan corroborated Allen's version of the story. "Ric was hanging Chianti bottles and [Mae] was laying tiles," Kogan said. "[But] Ike Sewell had great ambitions, and he loved to tell people he was the one who started pizza in Chicago." Sewell's widow, Florence, called Allen's claim preposterous.

In 1966, the ragtag group opened Gino's East, a maze of small, dark rooms with wooden booths that diners carved their initials into as a sign of loyalty. It immediately became Uno's and Due's chief rival. Generations of teenagers made it their first-date spot, then came back years later with children of their own in search of the initials they'd carved all those years ago over a soft, polenta-crusted sausage pizza and a Coke. Numerous Gino's outposts turned up around Chicago. In 2000, The Original Gino's East closed its flagship location and moved into a cavernous spot that once housed a Planet Hollywood—bringing the original Gino's booths and tables with them. There are now so many layers of graffiti etched in the wood, it looks like hieroglyphics.

For years, Adolpho ("Rudy") Malnati—Pizzeria Uno's bartender and an unofficial third partner—ran Uno's day-to-day operations along with his son, Lou. The two of them became the heart and soul of the operation. Rudy, a gregarious old man who spoke broken English and pinched the cheeks of children (not to mention the bottoms of women, according to most sources) was famously loyal to Sewell. So was Lou, a gruff, extroverted former marine.

In 1970, Lou, who was forty at the time, asked Sewell what was going to to happen to the business when he (Sewell) died. "There had never been anything on paper," says Marc Malnati, Lou's son. "So Lou asked if he could buy the piece that he thought

Courtesy of Pizzeria Uno

he owned." Sewell said no. So—stop us if this sounds familiar—Lou bailed to open his own pizzeria, leaving his own father behind. Rudy understood; Sewell did not. He never spoke to Lou again.

On March 17, 1971, the day Lou Malnati's opened, people lined the streets of Lincolnwood, a near north suburb. "It was as if no one in the suburbs had ever eaten pizza before," Marc Malnati says. When they got inside they realized another Chicago tradition had been born. It was a warm, homey place where football jerseys of Bears greats covered the walls—and the pizzas lived up to the hype. The tomato sauce came from vine-ripened plum tomatoes canned exclusively for Malnati's, and the cornmeal crust, while thinner than Uno's and Gino's, still reached the top of a two-inch deep-dish pan. In the years that followed, Lou Malnati's conquered Chicago's suburbs, replicating

Lou Malnati

its sports-and-deep-dish formula over and over again. Lou died of cancer in 1978, but his sons, Marc and Rick, now run the twenty-two area locations—and have made a cottage industry out of FedExing their father's famous pizzas all over the country. (They grossed $3.5 million in 2004.)

In the mid-seventies, trailblazing Chicago pizzerias such as Giordano's and Nancy's tweaked the Chicago style slightly by adding another layer of crust on top of the whole affair. These were the earliest stuffed pizzas, which looked more like pies than regular pizza ever did and took some of the pressure off the bottom crust. A few years later, Edwardo's, near the University of Chicago, took stuffed pizzas a step further by offering such un-pizza-like toppings as pesto, pineapple, and spinach. It was a major advance, and so many parlors followed suit that Edwardo's pies hardly qualify as exotica anymore.

In 2005, you can find deep-dish and stuffed pizza pretty much anywhere across the country. But Chicago will always be the mecca—and the old mansion housing Uno the shrine. When a place called Armand's opened in Washington, D.C., in 1975, the owner reportedly sent spies in the dead of winter to dive into the dumpster behind Uno's in search of clues about the famous recipe. They must have found something: There are now thirteen branches of Armand's in the D.C. area— and they all live and die by Chicago-style pizza.

Photos courtesy of Lou Malnati's Pizzeria

California

CALIFORNIA'S PIZZA HISTORY evolved differently than its brethren to the east. It wasn't Italian immigrants or smart marketers that created the next great wave—it was two forward-thinking chefs and one pizza-obsessed military brat. But the West Coast's unlikely culinary revolution was inevitable because of the area's built-in advantages: easy access to top-notch ingredients year-round; freedom from the shackles of tradition; scads of celebrities and the media buzz that surrounds them.

Alice Waters, the high priestess of "California cuisine," was an idealistic New Jersey native who graduated from The University of California-Berkeley in 1967 with a degree in French cultural studies. She spent a year in France, then taught at a Montessori school in the Bay Area and became infamous for hosting legendary dinner parties. In 1971, with a ten-thousand-dollar loan, Waters opened a little bistro in Berkeley called Chez Panisse. Her goal was seemingly simple: to cook a single, fixed menu of fresh, organic foods for her friends every night.

In an era when expensive San Francisco restaurants still served Camembert out of a can, that notion was nothing short of heresy. But Waters was on a mission. She constantly experimented and changed her seasonal menu, and she established relationships with local farmers, whom she pushed to grow ecologically sound food. She even hired a "forager" to seek out suppliers with an organic bent. Soon, Waters had a cult following in the Bay Area, where she was a good ten years ahead of the rest of California. Waters essentially kick-started the organic revolution from her unassuming wooden house in downtown Berkeley.

In 1980, she opened Chez Panisse Café upstairs, outfitted with a wood-burning brick pizza oven made by a local fireplace maker. It made perfect sense: The pies she churned out were in the same vein as the rest of her food—organic, fresh, simple. There was one pizza with pancetta, escarole, and hot pepper; another had wild nettles and Laughing Stock Farm pork sausage. She even served a calzone filled with goat cheese and chopped prosciutto, which prompted Craig Claiborne, the late *New York Times* food writer, to call Waters "one of the finest cooks in the country." Pizza had not only come of age, it had gone haute.

THE SAME YEAR that Chez Panisse Café opened, on the other side of the San Francisco Bay a twenty-five-year-old Washington state native named Ed LaDou was working as a pizza chef at Prego Ristorante. LaDou's colleagues had christened him "The Prince of Pizza," a title he had earned through years of exploring the pie's possibilities.

LaDou moved around a lot during his childhood—from Washington to Alabama to Hawaii to the Philippines—before landing in the Bay area in the mid-seventies.

The 12 pizzeria members at **THE CHEESE BOARD PIZZA COLLECTIVE** (Berkeley, California) decide as a group what pizza to make every day.

At the age of nineteen, he took a job at a pizzeria in Mountain View, California, called Frankie, Johnnie & Luigi Too. West Coast address notwithstanding, the owners had an East Coast mindset when it came to pizza. "The kitchen had pizza on one end of the line and sauté at the other end, which had wonderful fresh things to cook with," LaDou recalls. He just couldn't help himself; he started throwing all sorts of intriguing ingredients on pizza. A cult following adored his special giardiniera pizza (chopped up pepperoncini, eggplant, spinach, and Swiss cheese), but his old-school bosses thought it was weird and wouldn't allow any newfangled concoctions on the menu.

But at Prego, LaDou had access to better food-stuffs ("goat cheese and truffles and prosciutto and artichoke hearts and wonderful things like that") and a wood-fired oven—and this time the owners encouraged his experimentation. He tried everything with pizzas: He baked them. He sautéed them. He grilled them. He even tried frying them. On one night in 1980, LaDou made a pizza with pâté, ricotta, and roast asparagus and sent it out to a young couple near his station that was waiting to be seated. "The woman came over and introduced herself, then her boyfriend," LaDou recalled later. The woman was Barbara Lazaroff, and her boyfriend was Wolfgang Puck.

Puck, a charming thirty-one-year-old Austrian chef, had made a name for himself at the trendy Ma Maison in Hollywood and was planning his own restaurant concept, which he already knew would include a wood-burning oven built by the same craftsman who made the oven for Chez Panisse Café. Puck was so enthralled with LaDou's peculiar pizza that he flew him down to Los Angeles and offered him the pizzaiolo position at his upcoming restaurant. The place was called Spago, and in January 1982, it opened on Sunset Strip.

THE 8 BEST PIZZA NAMES IN AMERICA

① **THE BIG PIG** "Pepperoni, sausage, bacon, and ham. The cops who hang out here order it more than anybody." **(Picklefish in Mobile, Alabama)**

② **CARCASS** "All the meat we have topped with extra mozzarella" **(Pie-casso in Stowe, Vermont)**

③ **CLIFF CLAVEN** Marinated barbecue chicken, tomato, onion, Cheddar, jalapeños, and mozzarella on barbecue sauce **(Red Lodge Pizza Co. in Red Lodge, Montana)**

④ **COW TIPPER** Tomato sauce, mozzarella, ground beef, black olives, sheep's milk feta **(Lilly's in Raleigh, North Carolina)**

⑤ **DRAGON LADY** "A wicked blend of sun-dried tomatoes, onions, mushrooms, artichoke hearts, and capers" **(Old Town Pizza in Portland, Oregon)**

⑥ **GRIZZLY GULCH** Italian sausage, arti-choke hearts, feta, and mozzarella topped with fresh pesto or Wasatch marinara **(Wasatch Pizza Company in Salt Lake City, Utah)**

⑦ **LEANING TOWER OF PIZZA** Hamburger, pepperoni, pepperoncini, and onions **(Isles Pub & Pizza in Lincoln, Nebraska)**

⑧ **THE LITTLE WHITE LIE** White pizza covered in garlic butter and olive oil, topped with mozzarella, feta, white Cheddar, and Parmesan, sprinkled with black pepper and a blend of herbs and spices **(Christopher Pizza Co. in Nashville, Tennessee)**

SPAGO BLEW PEOPLE AWAY from the beginning. Puck's vision was a bold one: He wanted an eclectic mix of local products, border-bending dishes, and a casual-cool vibe. He got it all, starting on opening night, when a fleet of Rolls-Royces battled for parking out front. Spago, with its spectacular view and revolving display of contemporary art, quickly became the toughest reservation in the country, reportedly refusing three hundred reservations a day at its height.

It not only introduced Angelenos to a new blend of Asian and European influences, it also served as the de facto hangout for Hollywood's biggest stars. Most of them entered from the rear to avoid paparazzi, but refused to sit in the out-of-the-action back room, which was nicknamed "Siberia," because being *seen* at Spago was every bit as important as eating the food. And if Puck was brilliant in the kitchen, he was even better in the dining room, schmoozing with A-list celebrities until Spago's reputation—and his own—soared. With the stargazers and media constantly milling around, it wasn't long before the place was the most exciting restaurant in the country—and you didn't even have to wear socks.

Ed LaDou

Spago's open kitchen was a wonderland packed with exotic ingredients: scallops with roe, duck sausage, Santa Barbara shrimp—and LaDou's imagination was unleashed. Like a kid in a candy store, he would arrive at the restaurant before all the other cooks to get dibs on the first foods that arrived. He tried things no one had ever dared in the pizza world, playing with oil infusions and flavored doughs and sliding wild permutations of thin-crust pizzas into the wood-burning oven. "It was like being an artist who'd worked with ten colors all his life and then got to use three hundred," he said later.

Puck—who had fallen in love with wood-grilled pizzas at a friend's restaurant in the south of France—sensed an opportunity, and began pushing the new pizza inventions at Spago. No one knows how many movie deals were sealed over the famous salmon and dill crème fraîche creation.

Spago was a launching pad for an eventual Puck empire that includes a slew of restaurants across the country, a catering company, a line of gourmet packaged foods, a TV show, and a newspaper column. He was even on an episode of *The Simpsons.* As of 2003, Puck reported that all his commercial ventures grossed $170 million a year.

MEANWHILE, Ed LaDou remained behind the scenes while his boss's name became synonymous with gourmet pizzas. In 1983, LaDou decided it was time to move on. He liked Puck personally, but he was ready to start again, so he took his 250 pizza

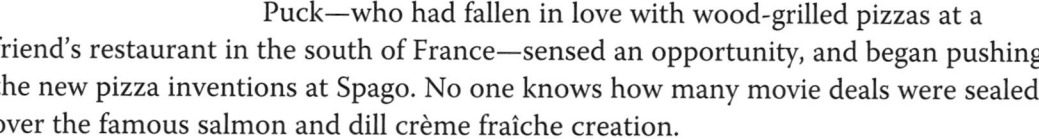

Courtesy of Caioti Pizza Cafe

A MATTER OF STYLE

There are so many regional styles of pizza—with so many precise variables—it's tough to keep them all straight.
Here's a primer on the 5 biggies.

New York

DEFINED A thin, chewy pizza generally made from high-gluten flour (usually 13.5–14.5 percent protein), high butterfat Grande mozzarella, San Marzano tomatoes, and New York's good old "hard" water **OVEN** Most often hearth or deck ovens (These days, the coal-fired ovens that made New York pizza famous are no longer being constructed because of environmental concerns—though certain places have been "grandfathered" in.) **TYPICAL TOPPING** Pepperoni **INNOVATOR** Gennaro Lombardi **TRADEMARKS** Floppy, foldable slices; yellow grease trails on the plate

Chicago

DEFINED A heavy pie made with a cornmeal-like crust that has been raised high on the sides of buttery deep-dish pans. The cheese is placed on the dough, the toppings on the cheese, and the chunky sauce (made with canned tomatoes) on top of everything. (Not to be confused with "stuffed" pizza, which has a second layer of dough on top—plus more sauce and cheese on top of that.) **OVEN** Gas **TYPICAL TOPPING** Sausage **INNOVATORS** Ike Sewell, Ric Riccardo Sr. **TRADEMARKS** Long cooking times; knife and fork a necessity; New Yorkers hate it

New Haven

DEFINED Free-form, hand-tossed "apizza" (pronounced "ah-beets") with crisp, often charred crust (thin but still doughier than New York pizza), and fresh tomatoes **OVEN** Coal-fired **TYPICAL TOPPING** "White clam" (grated cheese, whole clams, garlic, and oil; no tomato sauce or mozzarella) pizzas **INNOVATORS** Frank Pepe, Sally Consiglio **TRADEMARKS** Oblong shapes; in-fighting amongst proprietors

Neapolitan

DEFINED Tender/crisp pizzas with a high, blistered edge of crust, very little olive oil, non-liquid buffalo mozzarella, and peeled San Marzano tomatoes. The dough must be worked with the hands and placed on the surface of the oven (i.e., no pan). **OVEN** Wood-burning **TYPICAL TOPPING** Basil, garlic, and grated Parmesan **INNOVATOR** Raffaele Esposito **TRADEMARKS** Claims to be the only "true" pizza

California

DEFINED Light, airy thin-crust pizzas known for their offbeat (and often artisan) toppings. The dough is mixed until smooth, and often par-baked to order to keep it crispy. **OVEN** Wood-fired and often par-baked cheese **TYPICAL TOPPING** BBQ chicken; goat cheese with roasted peppers **INNOVATORS** Wolfgang Puck, Ed LaDou, Alice Waters **TRADEMARKS** Celebrity-tested, celebrity-approved

recipes and began work as a cooking instructor and caterer. "The truth is Wolfgang didn't know much about pizza at all, which is why he hired me," LaDou told Pizzamarketplace.com. "But all you have to do now is look in the grocery and see who still gets the credit."

One day, while preparing for a pizza-making class, LaDou was looking through his refrigerator for ingredients. He found a bottle of barbecue sauce, and decided to try it on a pizza. Eventually he added sliced chicken, cilantro, red onion, a little mozzarella, and some smoked Gouda. He liked the result, and added it to his recipe file. Not long after, one of LaDou's students introduced him to two Beverly Hills attorneys named Larry Flax and Rick Rosenfield. They were about to open an upscale pizzeria next to their office with backing from deep-pocketed investors such as Vegas mogul Steve Wynn. But their original chef had flaked out, and they didn't know a thing about cooking. They asked LaDou to come up with a menu, he pulled out his recipes, and three weeks later, on March 27, 1985, he was a minority partner when California Pizza Kitchen opened on Beverly Drive.

CPK was a bright, stylish two-thousand-square-foot restaurant with cheerful service, affordable prices, and an exhibition wood-fired pizza oven imported from Italy. The menu was full of plate-sized pizzas like no one had ever seen: Peking duck breast with hoisin sauce; Jamaican jerk chicken; marinated shrimp with fresh mint; and, of course, the now-famous barbecue chicken pizza.

This page: California Pizza Kitchen's famous barbecue chicken pizza; opposite page: Larry Flax (left) and Rick Rosenfield

Courtesy of California Pizza Kitchen

9 QUESTIONS FOR RICK ROSENFIELD,
CO-FOUNDER/CO-CEO OF CALIFORNIA PIZZA KITCHEN:

Did you start CPK on a shoestring?

We borrowed $250,000 to open it. But the day we opened in 1985, we put an "opening" sign—drawn on a poster board—in the window. We took down the sign when the first person walked in. That was Shirley MacLaine. Her office was nearby, and she walked in to try it.

Was it an instant hit?

It took off immediately. We tried to get flavors that people identified with—even if it was never on pizza before. Anything that works well on bread will work well on our pizza.

You grew up on Chicago pizza. How did you get into this thin gourmet stuff?

It was a California thing. I ended up in the Department of Justice in L.A., and so did my partner, Larry Flax. We started our law practice in 1973. We were white-collar federal criminal defense attorneys.

Where do the two of you fit into the history of California-style pizza?

The first California-style pizza—from a wood-fired oven with light and more exotic ingredients—was at Chez Panisse. So Alice Waters created it, Wolfgang Puck introduced it, and we sort of capitalized on it.

What was your goal?

When Puck introduced it to celebrities at Spago, you waited weeks to get in. Larry and I were thinking about a great chain of family restaurants. Our goal was less about pizza and more about a place where parents and kids can all go together and be happy.

Did you think it would be popular in regions used to heavier pizzas?

Bill Rice [former *Chicago Tribune* food writer] asked why we would want to bring this pizza to Chicago. I asked, "When was the last time you had Chicago pizza?"

"Ten years ago," he answered. "It's too heavy for me now."

I smiled. The following Sunday he wrote a great article about us in the *Tribune*.

Where did you get the crust recipe?

From Ed LaDou, the consultant we brought in. But Ed and Spago had sugar in the recipe. I changed the sugar to honey in the first week. So the crust recipe is part them and part us.

How many CPKs are there in the United States now?

141 is the answer today. By the time you print the book, there will be more. We grossed over $400 million in 2004.

What do you think when you see an offbeat pizza in a small town?

We are not looking for pizzas with incongruous tastes. Or pizzas that are creative for the sake of creativity. What we are looking for are pizzas that sound good and then deliver. I don't know of many pizzas that we have found in other pizzerias that made us say, "Boy, do we have to have that."

Courtesy of California Pizza Kitchen

LADOU GETTING HIS DUE

In the summer of 2005, Ed LaDou's contributions to shaping American cuisine were finally acknowledged—in a big way. The Smithsonian invited LaDou to do 2 pizza-making demos a day for *Food Culture USA*, its expansive celebration of the American artisan food revolution of the past 30 years. "As far as I know, this is the first time that pizza has been featured prominently on the national stage for its culinary merits," LaDou says.

It was another major step for pizza, further away from tradition—but closer to world domination. While the purists turned up their noses at the utter blasphemy of it all, pretty much everyone else loved the place. LaDou called it "volkspizza," or pizza for the people, and suddenly, the average Joe, unable to *buy* a reservation at Spago, could munch on a cheeseless Sichuan shrimp pizza with black Oriental mushrooms whenever he wanted at CPK.

Everyone was talking about the place. Ruth Reichl called the restaurant "gourmet fast food" in the *New York Times,* remarking, "The place seems born to be cloned." LaDou predicted in the *Los Angeles Times* that the barbecue chicken pizza was "probably going to be the most copied dish in the United States." Even Puck weighed in, though with a backhanded compliment. "I think it's flattering," he said in *Nation's Restaurant News.* "There's definitely room for an upscale Shakey's."

Reichl, it turns out, was most on the mark. California Pizza Kitchen outposts have spread like mad; there are now more than 145 full-service locations in the United

Courtesy of Caioti Pizza Cafe

States; the one in the Mirage Hotel and Casino in Las Vegas reportedly does more business per square foot than any other restaurant in the country. All told, the company grossed more than $300 million in 2004. It's safe to say that Flax and Rosenfield, the founders and CEOs, don't need to practice law anymore. And pretty much anywhere in the United States, you can find a place that's throwing some unlikely vegetable or sauce on a pizza—or making their own a barbecue chicken pizza.

But if you go on California Pizza Kitchen's Web site these days, you won't find Ed LaDou's name anywhere. He left in 1985 and sold his interest in the company a year and half later. "We parted amicably," LaDou says. "But there has been a cut-off from both of those companies [Spago and CPK]. They would both prefer to get the limelight for their pizzas instead of me." LaDou used the money to open his own little pizzeria in Laurel Canyon, California, called Caioti Pizza Cafe. He ran it for eleven years before moving into a slightly bigger space in Studio City, where he is quietly serving the same inventive pizzas he's always loved in a small neighborhood cafe decorated with pine wainscoting and old menus.

When LaDou sees combos that make no sense on a pizza, he can only shrug; his name may never be well known, but he's well aware of his influence on America's current pizza landscape. As writer Jonathan Gold wrote in *LA Weekly* in 1999: "If a pizza in Dayton, Ohio, has smoked Gouda and pine nuts on it, it is in no small part due to LaDou." ● ● ●

5 QUESTIONS FOR WOLFGANG PUCK

How did you get interested in pizza?
I grew up close to Italy but never liked their pizzas that much. In the early '70s, I lived in the south of France, and there was this place called Chez Gu with a wood-burning oven. The pizza was the only food we could afford.

And when you came to the United States . . . ?
. . . I tried some of the pizza chains and I said, "No, this is disgusting." In 1982, when I opened Spago, I decided to put the pizza oven in. But I didn't want to make pizzas like the Italians do; I wanted to make it our own style—or like the Italians in America.

And what was the reaction?
From the beginning, people loved these pizzas. After a year, I made one with mozzarella, fontina, goat cheese, and white truffles. The only complaint was the price: Some people said paying $30 for a pizza was crazy.

Smoked salmon pizza wasn't on the menu initially. How did people know to ask for it?
I started to send it to people [at their tables]. I sent it to Joan Collins and put some extra caviar on top. And I remember Robin Leach had it with champagne and baptized it as "the pizza of the rich and famous."

Do you think you've had a big impact on American pizza?
Not only pizza, but on casual restaurants having high-quality food. Places where the ambiance is casual but the food serious: something that fits into the California lifestyle.

Courtesy of 3 Tomatoes & a Mozzarella

CHAPTER 3
The Chain Gangs

WHEN PIZZA JUMPED FROM ITALY TO AMERICA, it never lost its initial culinary identity, but it did adapt to Anglo tastes. Gone in most cases was the original Neapolitan prototype, and in its place was an Americanized version: less garlic; oregano instead of basil; gas ovens instead of brick. Yet it wasn't until pizza broke out of the Italian-American neighborhoods of the East Coast and made its way to the suburbs and mid-sized towns in the Midwest that the United States really changed pizza. The change was not in form so much as in function: Where Italian immigrants saw the food of their childhood, businessmen in the Heartland saw dollar signs.

In the 1950s and 1960s, savvy entrepreneurs began to pick up on the marketing appeal of this flexible "new" dish, and they made it their boardroom plaything. This meant some major innovations—in particular, large-scale franchising and delivery. For better or worse, big business plucked pizza from relative obscurity and transformed it into the most profitable slice of the fast-food arena in the country and, soon, around the globe.

GOOD COCKTAIL PARTY ICEBREAKER

That circular white plastic thing that protects a delivered pizza from sticking to the inside of the box is called a package saver, and according to about.com, it was invented by Carmela Vitale of Dix Hills, New York. She filed for U.S. patent number 4,498,586 on February 10, 1983.

All this was much to the chagrin of the independent neighborhood joints, many of which, unable to compete with deep-pocketed corporations, went out of business. Worse, they were forced to watch as their treasured dish shifted from an individualized, authentic treat to a ubiquitous, mass-produced commodity with international clout. Italians may have brought pizza to the States, but America introduced it to the rest of the world.

THE ARC OF PIZZA in America at the end of the twentieth century can be encapsulated in one man's experience. He wasn't Italian, nor was he living in a large metropolitan area—nor was he particularly immersed in pizza's colorful history. Nor was he even an adult, at least not when he began. Frank Carney was a hardworking Kansas kid studying electrical engineering at the University of Wichita (now Wichita State University) and working five days a week at his family's grocery store in the late fifties. His father had died young but had left behind the corner grocery, which employed everyone in his large Irish-Scottish family. "We all worked multiple jobs," Carney says. "That was where we got the money to pay for school, buy our clothes, and do whatever we had to do."

In 1958, when Frank was nineteen, the beer joint in the funny little shack next to Carney's Market went belly-up. The landladies, who wanted a reputable business in the space, showed Frank's older brother Dan (a business student at the time) an article in the *Saturday Evening Post* about the popularity of New York pizza. "'How would you boys like to open a pizza place next door where the bar is?'" they asked, according to Carney. On the surface, it was a ridiculous idea. Neither of them knew the first thing about running a restaurant, and they were far from pizza experts: Dan had sampled it a few times while he was in the Air Force; Frank had eaten pizza as a side dish a few times at local Italian joints, and he simply thought it was "fun." But the possibility of owning their own business—the way their father had—excited them.

They enlisted the help of John Bender, an easygoing Air Force pilot who was employed at a nearby base. Bender, who lived in the same building as one of the Carney sisters, had worked at a pizza place in Bloomington, Indiana, and was looking for a part-time job to supplement his income. "He cooked pizza for my sister and her husband at his apartment," Carney says. "This was just when were thinking about going into the pizza business." He taught Frank, who had just finished his freshman year, and Dan, twenty-five, his recipe for thin-crust pizzas.

The Carneys borrowed six hundred dollars from their mother, bought some second-hand pizza equipment, and signed the lease. When it came time to name the six-hundred-square-foot place, their choices were limited: The sign they had inherited from the bar was

IDENTITY THEFT

A 2003 survey of 630 Domino's delivery drivers found that Paris Hilton was the most common fake name used by people calling for pizza deliveries. (John Ashcroft was #2.)

NEW YORK STYLE PIZZA

Courtesy of www.VintageMetalArt.com

so small, all they could fit on it was the word "Pizza" and maybe another three letters. Dan's wife, the story goes, took a look at the pointy roof. "It looks like one of those little huts up in the mountains," she said. Pizza Hut was born.

When the place opened in Wichita in the summer of 1958, its menu centered on Bender's crispy pizzas. "We only had eight toppings," Carney says, "but you could combine them any way you wanted." Word quickly got around town that a tiny place near the busy intersection of Kellogg and Bluff was serving something "new"—and tasty, to boot. After six months, business was so good that the Carneys and Bender decided to open another location. (Bender had been made a partner for three hundred dollars—perhaps the best investment of all time.)

Although it wasn't their original intention, the idea of expanding farther happened naturally. "There were franchises out there," Carney says. "This was back in the era of Holiday Inn. One of our managers wanted to have his own store. We didn't want to do that in Wichita because we wanted to have all the stores in Wichita. So he went to Topeka." The man paid a fee for the right to use the Pizza Hut name and its recipes and agreed on his territory, and the Carneys trained him personally. The new store was a success, and in dozens of new locations around the Midwest, they followed the same pattern over and over, offering stores to employees and friends first. The Pizza Hut franchise gold rush was on.

Pizza Hut became the brothers' life and livelihood, and eventually they both dropped out of college. "My mom was not pleased," Carney says. "But I was traveling too much. I had to stop taking classes." It turned out the Carneys had a knack for business and an unflagging entrepreneurial spirit—not to mention an inherently good product. In the sixties, Pizza Hut took off, with franchises opening extensively, efficiently, and absurdly fast, frequently focusing on small and medium-sized towns. One site was built from scratch at the Oklahoma State Fair in five days. (The national average is eighty-five days, per Pizza Hut's Web site.) Two years after the original opened,

PLUCK OF THE IRISH

Frank Carney isn't the only Irish kid from the Midwest who built a pizza empire. In 1960, around the same time that Pizza Hut was starting in Kansas, Tom Monaghan and his brother, James, put down $500 and bought a pizza store in Ypsilanti, Michigan, called DomiNick's. They got a 15-minute lesson in pizza making from Dominick himself and opened immediately. But James didn't want to quit his regular job as a mailman, and within a year he traded his half of the business to his brother—reportedly for a Volkswagen Beetle. As business took off, Tom developed a common-sense strategy: He opened stores near colleges and military bases and delivered hot pizzas within 30 minutes.

Eventually, Monaghan changed the name to Domino's and developed the familiar red-white-and-blue pizza boxes. "I decided we'd put 3 dots on the domino because we had 3 stores," Monaghan told *Fortune Small Business* magazine in 2003. "And every time we added one, we'd add a dot." In 1998, Monaghan sold Domino's for a reported $1 billion—most of which he gave to charity. There are more than 7,000 Domino's around the world. Good thing Monaghan stopped at 3 dots: Otherwise, that would have resulted in one hell of a box.

Everything for a complete pizza party

PIZZA PARTY! Skipper

Pizza Party Skipper pairs with the Pizza Hut brand

Photograph: Christopher Lowry

there were twenty-five stores, six of which the Carneys owned in Wichita; the rest were franchises. By 1968, the number of stores had ballooned to 310. Before the Carneys knew it, Pizza Hut was feeding a million people a week.

Pizza Huts of all shapes and sizes began to spread across the country in concentric circles—with centrally located Wichita at the nucleus. The Carneys, shrewd businessmen that they were, recognized that the restaurant needed a single, identifying look to create a strong brand. "It became a necessity to have an 'image building,' and so we had an architect do that for us," Carney says. "It started out as a cedar shake shingle roof in 1963, but that weathered and looked old." A professional group came in and overhauled the whole image, and the new look was a gabled building with a sloped red roof.

By 1971, all franchisees got the same standardized building, and Pizza Hut quickly grew into the biggest pizza restaurant chain in the world—sizewise and moneywise. "The reason we kept growing is no one figured out a reason to stop," Carney told the *Houston Chronicle* years later. And like McDonald's golden arches, in big cities and small towns alike, Pizza Hut's red roofs reached iconic status in American pop culture.

But as Frank's enthusiasm for the franchising business grew, Dan's began to wane. He was on the road all the time, and he missed his family; he did not enjoy the details of heading up an increasingly larger company. In 1973, Dan stepped aside, and Pizza Hut was Frank's to run. (John Bender had sold his stake in the business back in 1963 to go into the lumber business in southern Indiana, but he later became a Pizza Hut franchisee in Bloomington.)

Frank Carney promptly took a crash course in executive management. The college dropout must have been a good student, because the years that followed were Pizza Hut's heyday. During Carney's regime, the company became a franchising machine, experiencing the kind of astonishing growth that makes stockholders salivate and rivals shake their heads. "He wanted to grow Pizza Hut

Photograph: Matt Roberts © IFOCE

and we did," a franchisee named Bob Cressler told the *Wichita Business Journal* in 2001. "It was like hanging onto a comet going skyward."

It was difficult for potential franchisees to say no. Once Carney had them on board, he built up goodwill by encouraging them to take classes in any subject under the sun—whether business-related or not. In 1977, Pizza Hut was a billion-dollar-a-year company boasting 3,400 stores worldwide when Carney, with his stockholders' unanimous approval, sold it to PepsiCo for $300 million. In less than twenty years, his little six-hundred-dollar investment had increased in value by 5,000 percent.

FRANK CARNEY, of course, had more ambitious ideas. He was still Pizza Hut's president, but he was gunning for PepsiCo's top food operations spot, which would put him in charge of all its restaurant holdings (including a hot new acquisition called Taco Bell). But he was passed over for someone outside the company, and in 1980, just after helping to develop and roll out what would become Pizza Hut's most popular item, Pan Pizza (based on a meeting with Ike Sewell at Chicago's Pizzeria Uno), Carney left Pizza Hut.

In fact, despite numerous propositions from other pizza companies, Carney exited the business altogether, shifting his interests to venture capitalism. He invested the only way he knew how: big. He poured practically all his money into everything from ski resorts to oil to Chi-Chi's Mexican Restaurants, until he had almost doubled his net worth.

But in the late eighties the recession hit, and as the stock market fell, his investments began to tank. "They weren't all bad; they were just more bad than good," Carney says. "And I had a tendency to stay with them too long." By 1993, his fortune was gone. The same year, in Sao Paulo, Brazil, the ten-thousandth Pizza Hut unit opened, an occasion celebrated by soccer legend Pelé kicking a ball through the front door. The company Carney had founded and built had grown into an international juggernaut, featuring numerous styles of pizza—few of which were up to his standards. Carney believed that PepsiCo's desire for growth at all costs had left out one crucial

LAND SPEED RECORD

On June 19, 2004, at Bacci World Pizza Eating Championship in Downers Grove, Illinois, Sonya Thomas became the top pizza eater in the world. Thomas, a.k.a. "The Black Widow," ate 6 1/2 jumbo slices in 15 minutes—which may not sound like much, but each Bacci slice is 24 inches. (Afterward, she reportedly ate an Italian beef sandwich.) Thomas, who weighs 105 pounds, was the 2003 International Federation Of Competitive Eaters Rookie of the Year, and also holds competitive eating records in oysters, chicken wings, hard-boiled eggs, and countless other categories. She is single and lives in Alexandria, Virginia. (P.S.: Thomas did not compete in the 2005 competition, and lost her crown to Richard LeFevre, a 132-pound 60-year-old from Nevada.)

P I Z Z A DELIVERY DRIVERS

TELL GREAT STORIES OF HARDSHIP.

TO HEAR THEM TALK, YOU'D BELIEVE THEY WERE THE MOST POORLY TREATED SUBCULTURE OF WORKERS IN AMERICA — AND THEY COULD BE RIGHT.

HERE, FROM THE PEN OF CHICAGO-BASED ARTIST *JOHN KENZIE*, AN ILLUSTRATED GUIDE ON THEIR INJUSTICES.

PEOPLE WHO WANT TO HAVE A CONVERSATION WITH THE DRIVER

"NOW, DURKHEIM, HE USED A RADICAL FORM OF GUILD SOCIALISM ALONG WITH FUNCTIONALIST EXPLANATIONS, BUT MARXISM, ON THE OTHER HAND..."

PEOPLE WHO TIP ONLY THE LEFTOVER COINS

THAT'LL BE $44.50.

HERE'S $45. DON'T WORRY ABOUT THE CHANGE.

PEOPLE WHO BLAME HIGH PRICES ON THE DRIVER

18 BUCKS FOR A LARGE?

I DON'T MAKE THE PRICES. WHO AM I, ALAN GREENSPAN?

PEOPLE WHO SEND THEIR KIDS TO ANSWER THE DOOR

SIGH...

PEOPLE WHO PROMISE TO TIP NEXT TIME BUT NEVER DO

OH, I'M STRAPPED. I'LL GET YOU NEXT TIME.

YOU SAID THAT LAST TIME.

PEOPLE WHO BLAME THE DRIVER BECAUSE IT WAS LATE

DID YOU GET LOST?

HOW'D YOU GUESS?

element: quality. And even if he had wanted to return to the franchising business, there wasn't any territory that Pizza Hut's new owners had not already staked out.

PIZZA HUT STILL RULED THE ROOST, but by this point other mega-chains—such as Little Caesars and Domino's, two Michigan-based outfits that came of age in the 1960s—flooded the U.S. market and chipped away at the Hut's profits. Both had a strong identity: Little Caesar's was known for its goofy commercials, which featured a double-talking mascot clad in a toga. But Domino's in particular changed the game when it perfected the biggest pizza innovation to come along in years: delivery.

Where Pizza Hut was a family restaurant, a place to sit down and eat, Domino's set up shop near college campuses and promised to bring the pie to your door within thirty minutes—or it was free. "The thirty-minutes-or-free guarantee was as responsible for our growth as anything," Domino's founder Tom Monaghan told *Fortune* magazine years later. Domino's developed a sturdy, corrugated pizza box—and their delivery cars were easy to spot, with red-white-and-blue signs on top. In 1993, one of its drivers ran a red light and hit a woman in St. Louis, and a lawsuit followed. Monaghan insisted that delivering pizzas within thirty minutes was not about driving fast; it was about making the pizzas fast. A jury disagreed, and it cost Domino's $79 million. Shortly after, they discontinued the thirty-minute guarantee.

> **DONATOS,** a chain based in Columbus, Ohio, builds its pizzas on digital scales and weighs them and their ingredients to 1/100th of a pound.

8 CLEVER MARKETING PLOYS

① **INGLESIDE VILLAGE PIZZA (Macon, Georgia)** provides a lump of dough for kids to play with while waiting.

② Delivery drivers at the environmentally conscious **GALACTIC PIZZA (Minneapolis, Minnesota)** drive electric cars and wear superhero costumes that include lamé capes, sparkly jumpsuits, and go-go boots.

③ Inspired by a meter-long pizza the owner ate in Uruguay, **PINCH (New York, New York)** sells thin-crust pizza by the inch.

④ **PIZZA SCHMIZZA,** an Oregon-based chain, gave free slices to homeless people who agreed to hold up a sign that read "Pizza Schmizza paid me to hold this sign instead of asking for money."

⑤ **BEAU JO'S,** a chain in Colorado, challenges teams of 2 to finish a 12–14-pound Sicilian pizza: Those who do win $100 and become local legends.

⑥ **PIE IN THE SKY (Franklin, Tennessee)** uses a Chrysler Prowler as its rolling billboard.

⑦ **THE WEDGE PIZZERIA (Iowa City, Iowa)** invites customers to bring in anything they want to put on a pizza—no matter how weird—and they'll make it for you. ("We may even name a pizza after you if we like it enough.")

⑧ **SHAKESPEARE'S (Columbia, Missouri)** has long been known for snarky coupons with messages such as "Confused? Flustered? Lost track of what time it is? Call us! We have a clock! $1 off any large pizza."

10 GREAT PIZZERIA NAMES

1. **ESCAPE FROM NEW YORK PIZZA**
(Portland, Oregon)

2. **ZIMORINO'S RED PIES OVER MONTANA**
(Missoula, Montana)

3. **MOOSE'S TOOTH PUB & PIZZERIA**
(Anchorage, Alaska)

4. **PICKLEFISH**
(Mobile, Alabama)

5. **PIE-CASSO**
(Stowe, Vermont)

6. **PIZZA MY HEART**
(chain in California)

7. **PIZZA ORGASMICA**
(San Francisco, California)

8. **SOME GUYS PIZZA**
(Indianapolis, Indiana)

9. **TONY BOOMBOZZ PIZZERIA**
(Louisville, Kentucky)

10. **VINNIE VANGOGO'S**
(Savannah, Georgia)

THE FOURTH MEMBER of "The Big Four" was a young upstart making noise out of Louisville, Kentucky. Papa John's had its own rags-to-riches story: In 1984, its founder, John Schnatter, sold his old Camaro to buy a pizza oven and began selling pies from the former broom closet of his father's Jeffersonville, Indiana, tavern. His hand-tossed pizzas were so popular that he expanded and soon opened a store down the street. Within ten years, his company had relocated to Louisville and opened more than one thousand outlets around the country.

The spread of Papa John's may have been wide, but its focus was deliberately narrow: predominantly delivery and takeout of traditional pizzas made of fresh ingredients and a distinctively sweet sauce. Pizza Hut, meanwhile, further enlarged its menu to include hand-tossed, chunky-style, stuffed-crust pizzas—and even added Buffalo wings.

In 1994, Frank Carney got a call from a former Pizza Hut board member who was now a Papa John's franchisee. Convinced that Papa John's was the next wave, the man had switched teams—and he wanted Carney to take a look at the then ten-year-old chain. After some initial resistance, Carney agreed. When he arrived at Papa John's, he saw his future. "It wasn't payback, it was just a business opportunity that made sense," he said. "Houston was a market that I knew very well from Pizza Hut. But Pizza Hut has not always stayed with the highest quality that it could, so I thought this product could compete with what was out there at the time." Around the same time, Pizza Hut's head-quarters moved from Carney's hometown of Wichita to Dallas. That was the final straw: Carney mortgaged his home to pay for his own Papa John's franchise in Houston.

Schnatter and the rest of the young company felt lucky to get a man with Carney's franchising experience.

TRUMPED UP

The chain-pizza wars have only intensified over the years. Domino's Pizza reportedly paid between $2 and $4 million for a March 2005 episode of Donald Trump's NBC reality show, *The Apprentice*, in which the contestants were to create and market their own pizza. It was to be a big-time product placement for Domino's intended to boost the company's sagging profits.

But somehow a press release plugging the upcoming show landed at the Louisville corporate office of Papa John's—one of Domino's chief rivals. Papa John's rushed to buy up commercial airtime for the show, and John Schnatter, Papa John's founder, saturated prime-time airwaves with this line: "Why eat a pizza made by apprentices when you can call the pros at Papa John's?" It turned into a major coup for Papa John's. Meanwhile, the best thing the aspiring apprentices could come up with was Cheeseburger Pizza, which Domino's is now stuck with. Somehow, we doubt this would have happened if "The Donald" had been the CEO of Domino's.

And they were downright giddy over the fact that they'd scored the chief architect of their biggest rival—a fact they played up in a 1997 commercial in which Carney shows up at a fictional Pizza Hut meeting wearing a Papa John's shirt. "Sorry, guys," he tells the shocked franchisees. "I found a better pizza." His decision to join "the enemy" ruffled plenty of feathers among Pizza Hut brass, a subject that rankled the normally genial Carney. "All of those guys are worth millions now," he told the *Houston Chronicle* in 1997. "If I am taking bread off their tables, I'd like to know which condo or summer home they are talking about."

Over the years, the competition between Pizza Hut and Papa John's has been pretty ugly. According to a *Los Angeles Times* story in 2000, Pizza Hut employees were known to secretly follow Papa John's drivers to give Pizza Hut coupons to customers who had just ordered from their rival. For their part, Papa John's employees reportedly parked their trucks in front of Pizza Hut restaurants and handed out free pizzas to customers about to enter. Not to be outdone, Pizza Hut put Papa John's name on doormats, mini-punching bags, and even, for a time, on the toilet bowl of the corporate jet. "The odds of Papa John's beating Pizza Hut were ludicrous," Carney said. "I studied the market and I knew they could co-exist and both be successful." Nevertheless, there have been accusations flying back and forth, lawsuits over commercials and slogans, and bad blood galore. Whether we're talking billion-dollar corporations or mom-and-pop pizzerias, pizza seems to bring out the fight in people.

CARNEY, who still resides in Wichita, now runs 131 Papa John's franchises in five markets, including his hometown. In 1998, he went back to Wichita State University to finish his degree—in business, of course; now, he routinely gives talks to college classes.

PAULINE'S PIZZA (San Francisco, California) grows its own organic fruits and vegetables—and bottles its own wine from locally grown organic grapes.

"I tell them, 'You don't have to know exactly where you're going when you start,'" he says. "We didn't have the idea, we didn't know how to make pizza, and we didn't have any money. You just need desire and the spark."

Ironically, his new company has experienced the kind of unbridled growth he railed against at Pizza Hut under PepsiCo. According to *Pizza Marketing Quarterly*, as of January 2005 Papa John's had 2,825 restaurants (570 company-owned and 2,255 franchised) operating in forty-nine states and twenty international markets—plus 117 Perfect Pizza restaurants in the United Kingdom. And it has also beefed up its menu to include such items as Buffalo wings and chicken strips—and pizzas as far-flung as Hawaiian barbecue. At press time, because of increased competition, the development of Papa John's had slowed considerably.

AMERICA'S OLDEST DELIVERY BOY

8 QUESTIONS FOR PIZZA SCHMIZZA EMPLOYEE ROGER JEHAN, 76, THE OLDEST PIZZA DELIVERY BOY IN THE UNITED STATES:

What did you do before delivering pizzas?
I was a tool and die maker. Then I retired in 1975. The store opened in 1993, and I came every morning to clean up the store. Now I'm strictly delivery for 1 store. My son's store.

How did you get the job?
My son told his mother and I that he was going to open a pizza place in Hillsborough [Oregon]. And I said, "Pizza schmizza. Get a job." That's where the name came from.

Your son is your boss?
Oh, yes. As the Mexican workers here say, *El Patron*.

Is being a delivery boy a promotion for you?
Before I used to do everything in the store. They couldn't afford me. Now I do 20 hours, 5 days a week. I don't work Saturday or Sunday; it's against my religions. I don't know which religion. I have a few of them.

How's the pay?
Not bad. Same for all 14 years. We don't want to change anything.

Courtesy of Roger Jehan

What's the worst tip you ever got?
Once I got 2¢. I can't remember where. Maybe I don't want to remember where. You have to take it with a grain of salt.

And the best?
We had one from Intel that was a 2-day affair: 304 pizzas and 304 2-liters. I think we got about $600 in tips on that one.

What have you learned?
Sometimes when we have a family who comes in with a little child who makes a lot of noise, I say, "Give him a glass of red wine. He will be asleep in a minute."

Courtesy of www.VintageMetalArt.com

> "There's no better feeling in the world than a warm pizza box on your lap."
> —actor Kevin James

Carney has softened his stance toward his old company. "There's no animosity on my side," he says. "I've got a lot of respect for the Pizza Hut company and operators. They've done a great job." Pizza Hut, now a subsidiary of Yum! Brands, Inc., currently operates in one hundred countries and territories around the world. And it has even grander designs for the future. In 2000, Pizza Hut put its logo on the world's largest proton rocket, and the next year, it "delivered" pizza to astronauts living on the International Space Station. From Kansas to outer space in forty-one years: Now that's expansion. ●●●

Courtesy of Home Run Inn

CHAPTER 4

'Za 'Za Boom

IF THERE'S ONE THING Americans love more than pizza, it's convenience. The sheer number of remote controls and cell phones and flat-screen televisions in our SUVs attest to that fact. This desire for comfort carries over into the pizza world, too: Who among us hasn't had a couple of large pies delivered during the Super Bowl? Pizza Hut recently hooked up with Sony, enabling those who play an online game called EverQuest II to order a pizza—using their keyboard. (As if the phone wasn't convenient enough.) Big business has sought out every way possible to bring pizza into every American's home—but delivery is only part of the equation.

Opposite page: The kitchen that spawned a frozen empire—Home Run Inn, circa 1947

THE FIRST FROZEN PIZZAS that Celentano Brothers put on supermarket shelves in 1957 had little in common with the stuff being churned out in restaurants at the time. Ice crystals destroyed the dough's gluten composition—not to mention the cell structure of the toppings, which ended up releasing water when thawed.

PIZZA PORN

In 2004, at the height of drugs such as Viagra, Levitra, and Cialis, a British supermarket chain announced its plans to unveil an "aphrodisiac pizza" called "Pizzagra." It contained artichoke, asparagus, ginger, chocolate, strawberry, banana, and other items "renowned for their ability to lift the libido in both men and women."

The result was a mushy crust and dry toppings. (An early homemade Chef Boyardee "box" pizza with canned sauce and Parmesan cheese wasn't much better.) But the first grocery store versions were surprisingly popular. By 1969, another early frozen pizza, Totino's, had penetrated 75 percent of the market, proving a valuable point: The pizza market was endless, and pizza makers had barely begun to tap it.

When Senator John Heinz III asked Delores Revello, matron of **REVELLO'S PIZZA** (Old Forge, Pennsylvania), "How do you make the cheese?" she retorted, "How do you make your ketchup?"

In 1962, Pep and Ron Simek (pronounced "Shimmick"), two brothers in Medford, Wisconsin, were running a small, quiet bar bordered by a cemetery. Ron, a former lumberjack, lived with his family in the back of the tavern; his six-foot-by-six-foot kitchen doubled as the bar's kitchen. One night, after a few beers, Pep, the more outgoing of the two, began to cut dangerously loose on the beer-soaked floor. "He started dancing the Peppermint Twist to the jukebox in the bar," Ron told *Fortune* years later. "Next thing you know, he was on the floor with a broken leg." Incapacitated, Pep spent most of the winter in the tiny kitchen playing around with pizza recipes, limping out in his cast to give away the more successful creations to bar patrons.

The combination he finally settled on, with a balanced mix of five spices, was well received, and the Tombstone Tap began to fill up. Sensing they were onto something, the Simeks got their wives involved. Together, the two couples made one hundred extra pies a week, which they then froze, carried in a cooler, and sold at other bars in the area. Beer-drinking Wisconsinites, they found, loved these Tombstone pizzas with their brews. Soon business was going so well, Pep and Ron purchased a freezer truck that could hold 1,800 pizzas. But they outgrew that in a hurry, too. In 1970, the brothers purchased land in Medford to build a factory in a vast industrial park where they could produce pizza exponentially faster.

Frozen pizza becomes an American tradition

Courtesy of Home Run Inn

The Simeks, thrilled with their success, continued to sell pizza to taverns, gas stations, and bowling alleys, eventually adding small independent grocery stores and, finally, major supermarket chains. By the mid-eighties, what had started as a cottage industry had become one of the largest frozen pizza manufacturers in America, with more than $100 million in sales. In 1986, the Simeks, fed up with the politics of their suddenly major corporation, sold Tombstone to Kraft Foods, Inc., the food giant based in suburban Chicago, and walked off with a bundle in the deal.

Today, Ron is retired out west; Pep still lives in Medford, Wisconsin, and has gone back to producing his own personal line of frozen pizzas, Pep's, which are sold all over his home state. "We're back to using the original recipe," Pep told the Wausau (Wisconsin) *Daily Herald* in 2003. "They [Kraft] changed the original all to hell. I don't eat their sausage. It's got a lot of soy protein and . . . I don't want to talk about it."

The Tombstone story is just one of many. In the eighties and nineties, every major food firm—including Quaker Oats, Pillsbury, and General Mills—bought out smaller companies that supplied frozen pizza to supermarkets. Other corporations began their own operations that would capitalize on pizza's adaptability. Most of them got rich as frozen pizza became one of the most popular supermarket items in America.

Once you factored in the ever-growing influence of chain pizzerias, it was safe to say that the balance of power in the pizza world had officially shifted from dough-tossing, peel-brandishing pizzaioli to brand managers

7 MEMORABLE PIZZA MOMENTS IN MOVIES

① **SATURDAY NIGHT FEVER (1977)**
Scene John Travolta struts down a Brooklyn street eating 2 slices of pizza on top of each other, folded over—the ultimate ad for New York pizza. **Verdict** Good dancing, good pizza.

② **DO THE RIGHT THING (1989)**
Scene Pizza is almost a character in Spike Lee's film, which stars Lee as a pizza deliveryman in a pizzeria fraught with racial tension. **Verdict** Good movie, bad rep for pizza parlors.

③ **E.T. (1982)**
Scene Henry Thomas gets a pizza delivered to his suburban home, only to step on the box because he's discovered an alien in the tool shed. **Verdict** Good movie, waste of a pizza.

④ **MYSTIC PIZZA (1988)**
Scene This coming-of-age tale, which kick-started the career of Julia Roberts, takes place in a Connecticut fishing village pizzeria famous for its special sauce. **Verdict** Chick flick, good pizza.

⑤ **FAST TIMES AT RIDGEMONT HIGH (1982)**
Scene A spaced-out Sean Penn infuriates his history teacher by getting a pizza delivered to the classroom. **Verdict** Good movie, saggy pizza.

⑥ **SPIDER-MAN 2 (2004)**
Scene Tobey Maguire, as a pizza deliveryman, swings from skyscraper to skyscraper with pizzas in tow as his 29-minute delivery guarantee ticks away. **Verdict** Good special effects, bad pizza.

⑦ **GOODFELLAS (1990)**
Scene Mafia goombahs threaten to shove a mailman's head into a pizza oven if he keeps delivering letters to Henry Hill's home that prove the aspiring mobster has been ditching school. **Verdict** Didn't actually see any pizza, but that old oven looks authentic.

and marketing directors. Most of the moneymen didn't know a pizza peel from a banana peel, but they were well versed in such things as demographics and "lifestyle choices," and that was where the opportunity was.

If there is one thing the purists hate more than the proliferation of chains, it's frozen pizzas. To hear them tell it, what was once an art form—the preparation of a perfect pie using fresh ingredients and years of training—has been co-opted by major corporations with dollar signs in their eyes. The corporations, they argue, employ assembly lines to mass-produce look-alike pizzas that they freeze and foist off on the unsuspecting masses. To the independent pizza maker whose family recipe had been

> "A good slice of pizza can be as good as a $200 meal in any restaurant."
>
> —actor Benicio Del Toro

10 GREAT PIZZA WEB SITES

ABOUTPIZZA.COM Glossy, professional site dripping with history, recipes, and links galore.

ENCYCLOPIZZA
www.correllconcepts.com/Encyclopizza/_home_encyclopizza.htm
Basically an online pizza reference book in 13 chapters.

PIZZATODAY.COM
Well-archived Web site of the popular Louisville-based monthly magazine; features in-depth stories, a vendor directory, and a weekly newsletter.

PIZZATHERAPY.COM
A cheery, if lo-fi, repository for all things pizza. The list of readers' favorite pizzas around the nation is entertaining and helpful.

TIPTHEPIZZAGUY.COM
Edifying pages about how to make delivery drivers' lives bearable. The message boards, full of drivers' pet peeves, are worth the price of admission.

PMQ.COM *Pizza Marketing Quarterly*'s business-savvy site has a wonderful "Ask the Experts" section with scores of helpful hints on how to run your own pizzeria.

QUARTERBYTE.COM/BRIAN/BRICKOVEN.HTML
One man's saga of building a brick oven in his backyard, complete with cartoons illustrating the "Stored Heat Masonry Oven Theory."

SLICENY.COM The definitive blog for current New York pizza information—it's funny, opinionated, and vast (just like New York).

WWW.RECIPESOURCE.COM/MAINDISHES/PIZZA
A digital recipe Rolodex that includes hundreds of straightforward pizza options.

PIZZAMARKETPLACE.COM
Serious-minded site with industry news, including niche business features like a "cheese market analysis."

lovingly passed down for generations, these cardboard pretenders represent nothing short of sacrilege.

But to the people who consume them hand over fist, they are an American tradition. Sure, the crust and cheese are chewy, and the sauce isn't as zingy as a restaurant's—but it looks like pizza, it smells like pizza, and it tastes like pizza (sort of). So where is the shame in that? Generally speaking, the American family that needs to get its young children fed quickly and economically has always been more interested in convenience than authenticity. Why go out for pizza, they reason, when we can eat it in our own home? And why spend an hour waiting for the delivery guy when we can pop a pizza in the oven for fifteen minutes, pay considerably less, and make everyone happy? "In other words, they were cheap and children liked them," Curt Wohleber wrote in *Invention & Technology* in 2005. "So did parents, especially since they didn't have to eat them."

By the time Kraft bought Tombstone in 1986, the options lining the frozen-food shelves were endless. Totino's had patented a crust that could withstand freezing and still remain crisp. Ubiquitous brands such as Tony's, Jack's, and Red Baron—and countless other competitors offering French bread pizzas, microwaveable pizzas, and pizza rolls—had shoppers scratching their heads, wondering what the difference was between them all. But they must not have been too concerned, because they spent nearly $1 billion a year on frozen pizza.

Then, in 1995, Kraft fired the Shot Heard 'Round the Frozen Pizza World. After years of top-secret scientific experiments, it finally unveiled DiGiorno, a technological breakthrough with a "self-rising" crust that imitated the gold standard: hand-tossed pizza. For the first time, any regular pizza fan could take a frozen pizza and cook it up *fresh* in his own home. DiGiorno's original business objective didn't involve chipping away at other frozen pizzas' profits (after all, Kraft still owned Tombstone and Jack's)—but rather taking a bite out of the huge pizza delivery market. If DiGiorno could get shoppers to say, "Wow, this tastes like a fourteen-dollar pizza, and it only costs six bucks," then Kraft would have a huge hit on its hands. An instantly catchy slogan, "It's not delivery, it's DiGiorno," made their goal clear.

YADA YADA YADA . . .

Seinfeld has always had a thing for pizza. From Kramer heating up his clothes in the Paisanos oven, to Elaine marveling over her stuffed crust, to George's desperate attempts to keep his high score on the Frogger machine at his childhood pizzeria, the show's love affair with the pie is well documented. But the most inspired moments involve Kramer's idea for a pizzeria where customers can make their own pizzas. George scoffs, reminding him it's not prudent to have untrained people shoving their arms into a 600° oven, but Kramer, undeterred, convinces Poppie, an incontinent restaurateur, to go into business.

They begin making a test pizza, and all is going well . . . until Kramer decides to put cucumbers on his pizza, angering his old-school partner. The argument deepens, leading to theological questions about what constitutes a pizza and when it becomes one (Kramer claims it's a pizza the moment it comes out of the oven; Poppie says it's as soon as you put your hands in the dough). It seems that even on TV, pizza's culture war rages on.

Suddenly, the black-and-white frozen pizza market was in Technicolor, and sales figures went wild across the board. The overall sales for frozen pizza more than doubled within two years, and, in short, people were finally buying frozen pizzas because they tasted *good*. Even the most hardened pie man had to admit that a frozen pizza with self-rising crust was considerably closer to a "real" pizza. Other companies, concerned that their old products with par-baked crust had been rendered obsolete, began working on their own self-rising products. When the Schwan Food Company introduced Freschetta with a rising crust that it claimed tasted like artisan-made bread, a lawsuit from Kraft followed, alleging corporate spying and stealing trade secrets. The case settled out of court in 2001.

Now, the U.S. frozen pizza market is closing in on an astounding $5 billion in sales. DiGiorno is still number one, but it shares the shelves with scores of new-and-improved frozen pizzas (even Pep's offers a self-rising crust option) that make the old versions seem outrageously antiquated. Ever the innovator, Kraft recently added a pizza with a self-rising crust that need only be microwaved for a few minutes. And number two? It's Freschetta, thanks to a new product that emulates the flavor of brick-oven pizza. Guess all's fair in love, war, and pizza.

WHILE THE GIANT CHAINS and food companies were entrenched in corporate warfare, a new luxurious option slipped in under the radar in the nineties: "Take-and-bake" pizza.

The largest take-and-bake purveyor, the Vancouver, Washington-based Papa Murphy's, offered the best of both worlds: a partially baked, restaurant-quality pizza that you could pick up nearby and make in your own home. The company's franchises, which now number more than eight hundred, feel a lot like Subway, the sandwich chain. Customers watch an employee custom-make their pie with fresh ingredients behind a sneeze-guard glass—then they take home a partially cooked pizza on a special tray that guarantees a crispy crust when baked in a home oven. Anyone who has ever complained that his delivered pizza is lukewarm has only himself to blame if he screws up a Papa Murphy's pie.

At press time, Papa Murphy's had grown into the sixth-largest pizza chain in the country. And there is plenty of room on the bandwagon. Scores of other take-and-bake operators have hopped on from coast to coast, led by groups such as Figaro's Italian Pizza, Nick-N-Willy's, and Mom's Bake At Home Pizza (which reportedly began selling gourmet take-home pizzas as early as 1981 in Philadelphia). The industry is exploding at the moment, and for good reason.

From a business standpoint, take-and-bake pizza shops are pure gold. Proprietors keep operating costs to a minimum, because they require less equipment (no ovens,

Vincent Chianese, owner of **VINCENT'S PIZZA PARK** (Pittsburgh, Pennsylvania), on the secret ingredient in his pizza: "Customers claim I put cigarette ashes in it."

11 GREAT CHILDREN'S BOOKS ABOUT PIZZA

① **HI, PIZZA MAN!** by Virginia Walter (1995): A little girl, waiting for her pizza, imagines the driver as various domesticated and non-domesticated animals, the poor guy. ("Woof woof, pizza dog!")

② **HOLD THE ANCHOVIES!** by Shelley Rotner and Julia Pemberton Hellums (1996): An easy step-by-step explanation of how pizza is made—from picking the grain to sliding the pie into the oven. With great photos and a recipe.

③ **LITTLE NINO'S PIZZERIA,** by Karen Barbour (1987): Heartwarming story about a boy who loves his father's modest restaurant. Bonus points for colorful illustrations and subliminal warning about the dangers of expanding operations.

④ **THE RATTLEBANG PICNIC,** by Margaret Mahy (1994): Hilariously absurd tale involving a volcano, an ill-fated picnic, and Granny McTavish's pizzas—which are so overcooked they can be used as car wheels.

⑤ **LITTLE RED HEN MAKES A PIZZA,** by Philemon Sturges (1999): The titular feathered character in this zany story asks her neighbors (a duck, dog, and cat) to help make a pizza, only to be rebuffed. She shares anyway—and they happily do the dishes. Neat cut-paper illustrations.

⑥ **PIZZA PAT,** by Rita Golden Gelman (1999, 2005): Brand-new readers love this sing-songy story about Pat, a seasoned pizzaiolo who makes a wood-fired pizza from scratch only to have a legion of neighborhood mice run away with it.

⑦ **THE PRINCESS AND THE PIZZA,** by Mary Jane and Herm Auch (2002): In this giddy fairytale send-up, Paulina attempts to make a delicious pizza to win the hand of the prince. She is successful, of course—but opts instead to open a pizzeria.

⑧ **HOW PIZZA CAME TO QUEENS,** by Dayal Kaur Khalsa (1989): This story about an elderly Mrs. Pellegrini—and how she introduced pizza to a neighborhood—is so nostalgic (and Khalsa's kaleidoscopic paintings are so eye-popping), it's easy to forgive the historical inaccuracies.

⑨ **YOUNG CAM JANSEN AND THE PIZZA SHOP MYSTERY,** by David A. Adler (2000): Cam loses her jacket in a pizzeria that makes "the best pizza in the world" (which, apparently, is in a mall). Relying on her photographic memory, she—and the reader—attempt to find the jacket.

⑩ **PETE'S A PIZZA,** by William Steig (1998): Pete is bummed because it's raining and he can't play ball, so his dad cheers him up by "turning him" into a pizza. ("Pizza makers are not supposed to tickle their pizzas!")

⑪ **PIZZA FOR SAM,** by Mary Labatt (2003): A hungry dog with an aversion for dog food discovers the joys of the pie in this book for beginning readers.

8 QUESTIONS FOR TONY GEMIGNANI

Standing on the shoulders of display spinners in the 1980s—such as Barry O'Halloran and Dolphis Boucher—Gemignani, 32, is a 6-time world pizza-throwing champion, coach of the U.S. Pizza Team, and co-owner of Pyzano's (Castro Valley, California).

How did you first get interested in throwing pizza?
My brother Frank taught me the basic toss at Pyzano's in 1991. I thought that was kind of boring, so when kids came into the restaurant, I would do tricks for them.

When did you start entering competitions?
In 1995 I entered my first competition for the best pizza thrower in the world—and I won. I ended up winning in 1995, 1996, and 1997. Then in 2000, I went to the World Pizza Championship in Italy. I won that year—and in 2001.

Jeez. How could you top that?
Pizza Marketing Quarterly and I created the U.S. Pizza Team in 2001. I was the coach, and I trained everyone in the U.S. who came out to compete. We would scout food conventions and find the best and take them to Italy every year.

What are you up to now?
I stepped away from the U.S. team and created a new team in 2004: The World Pizza Champions. They are the best acrobats and bakers and makers in the U.S. The fastest [dough spinners] and biggest [meaning they can stretch the largest skin]. We travel all over the world doing acrobatic shows.

What's your best trick?
It's called the Gemignani. Instead of across my shoulders, one way, I do 2 across, in opposite directions. Jay Leno called us the Harlem Globetrotters of pizza. What they do with basketball, we do with pizza.

What is the point of all this?
Mostly for show, but I think it's taking what we do to another level. You always want to get better at what you do. And when you are an independent pizza operator going against Pizza Hut and Domino's, you don't have the power to do a national TV commercial. I have been able to get millions of dollars of free advertising by being on Jay Leno and CNN and the Food Network.

Isn't all this a waste of dough?
I use ProDough, a fake dough that I came out with for people to practice with.

Why is everyone so obsessed with watching people toss pizza?
A lot of adults think of it from when they were younger and they remember that guy in the window in their old neighborhood. And kids look at it as the greatest thing in the world. It captivates everyone.

Courtesy of Tony Gemignani

no boxes, no tables). As a result they can afford to sell pizzas at considerably lower prices than, say, Domino's. And a sizeable percentage of Papa Murphy's profits have always come from families on food stamps and assistance programs, who are able to spend their benefits at take-and-bake places since such establishments qualify as deli stores rather than restaurants. The company's pizzas may be half-baked, but the concept isn't.

THE REMARKABLE thing about the pizza world (where the dish's definition depends on who and where you're asking) is that there's room for everyone. The skilled artisan can spend years honing her craft in pursuit of the perfect traditional Neapolitan pie, and find great acclaim in the process. Meanwhile, for those with no ties to the past who don't see pizza as a fixed idea, but rather as a starting point from which to display creativity, the sky is the limit. The dish is enough of a chameleon that it can support all brainstorms—a fact that has led to a proliferation of unlikely variations that differ greatly from the classic Neapolitan version.

You can forgo the cheese (New Haven's famous white clam pie); use substitutes for tomato sauce (Ed LaDou's barbecue sauce and pesto experiments at California Pizza Kitchen and Spago); or even skip the bread altogether (Donato's low-carb version). Others serve the familiar ingredients in a different form: Shortstop Deli is legendary in Ithaca, New York, for "Poor Man's Pizza," a made-to-order pizza sub on French bread that gets popped into an oven for a few minutes. DoubleDave's Pizzaworks, a popular Texas chain, has "Peproni Rolls," pizza crust rolled around pepperoni and provolone. And in Chicago, D'Amato's pizza bread is a popular permutation. Others specialize in panzerotti (deep-fried pizza) or "pizza chips," and calzones—basically a folded and stuffed crust—are everywhere. The variations go on and on.

Pizza has evolved so much you can put whatever toppings you want on practically anything that passes for bread (matzo, English muffins, pita) and still, technically, call it a pizza. The peanut butter and pepperoni number at the California-based John's Incredible Pizza Co. may sound like an unappealing combination, but it's successfully marketed and sold from Fresno to Victorville every day. PieWorks, a gourmet chain in the South, touts its 150 toppings—from jellybeans to Spam—as a selling point. These days, no one bats an eye at the taco pizza in Antlers, Oklahoma (High Street Pizza); Thai pizza in Laramie, Wyoming (Grand Avenue Pizza); crawfish tail-cream cheese-red pepper pizza in Ridgeland, Mississippi (Amerigo); or alligator pizza all over Oregon (Pizza Schmizza).

Patrons of Pizza Schmizza (Oregon) can enjoy the kooky atmosphere as well as an alligator-topped pizza

Courtesy of Pizza Schmizza

Despite all this experimentation, pepperoni is still the king—in the United States, that is. Elsewhere, you're more likely to find red herring (Russia) or coconut (Costa Rica). The word "pizza" is now a part of pretty much any language spoken on earth, and the variations you'll find in foreign countries say as much about the people who live there as pepperoni says about Americans. [See page 15 for the most popular pizza toppings around the world.]

Rosario Buonassisi, one of the foremost pizza experts in the world, has defined pizza as "a thin layer of leavened dough, ideally disk-shaped, made by thoroughly kneading wheat, flour, yeast, salt, olive oil, and water, and then covering with various ingredients before being baked in an oven." Notice he says nothing about cheese or tomatoes. By Buonassisi's definition, every single one of the aforementioned variations has just as much right to call itself a pizza as does a classic Margherita. To put it mildly, this is not an opinion shared by all.

In many ways, pizza now finds itself stuck in a vicious cycle. The further it drifts from its original form, the less people associate it with Italy—and the less "Italian" it becomes, the more people feel free to alter it. The result: Pizza, despite its popularity, is suffering an international identity crisis. And when a dish experiences the kind of growing pains that pizza has—undergoing such dramatic changes since 1889—you can't help but wonder about its future.

That's exactly what happened in Naples, the birthplace of modern pizza. In 1984, a small group of Neapolitan pizzeria owners, concerned about what their town's most famous export had become, formed the *Associazione Verace Pizza Napoletana* (VPN). Their mission is to protect and preserve traditional standards for pizza, according to the following stringent guidelines:

- The dough must be made only with flour, salt, water, and natural yeast (or brewer's yeast).
- The dough must be kneaded by hand or by mixers that do not cause the dough to overheat (no rolling pins).
- The dough must be punched down and shaped by hand.
- Pizza may be made only in wood-burning, bell-shaped brick ovens.
- Pizza must be cooked on the surface of the oven (no pan, no container).
- Pizza must be cooked at a temperature of at least 750° F.
- Only four pizza variations are allowed:
   1) *Margherita* (tomato, olive oil, Parmesan, and mozzarella);
   2) *marinara* (tomato, olive oil, oregano, and garlic);
   3) *formaggio e pomodoro* (tomato, olive oil, and grated Parmesan); and
   4) *ripieno* (a calzone filled with ricotta or mozzarella, olive oil, and salami).

LEDO PIZZA (Annapolis, Maryland) throws away any dough not used within 2 hours. If it's not used within 2 hours, it's gone. "There are timers in every store," says Ledo's CEO, Rob Beall.

This definition of "real" pizza is obviously more narrow than Buonassisi's more inclusive one, ruling out the bulk of America's sixty thousand-plus pizzerias in one fell swoop. The VPN petitioned the Italian government to have Neapolitan pizza recognized as a "DOC" *(denominazione di origine controllata)* product, a designation that Chianti and prosciutto di parma had enjoyed for years. This would protect Neapolitan pizza and make it the governmental standard by which all pizzas are judged. In 1998, the VPN got its wish. The city of Naples now has a logo that pizzerias hang in their window if they serve "true" Neapolitan pizza. Although the organization has granted VPN membership to pizzerias from Japan to Brazil, it's safe to say that Neapolitans officially want their dish back.

THE WORLD ACCORDING TO CHRIS BIANCO

Pizza aficionados don't speak of Chris Bianco, the single-minded owner of Phoenix's Pizzeria Bianco: They rhapsodize. Bianco represents the new breed of pizzaiolo who lives for pizza, dies for pizza, and probably dreams of pizza—a passion that shows at his restaurant. "He's amazing," says John Arena, owner of Metro Pizza in Las Vegas. "He won't allow people to take pizzas out of the restaurant. If you want to change something, he'll tell you to leave rather than do it. He simply won't compromise his vision of what a pizza is supposed to be." A legendary Bianco story involves a customer asking Bianco why he wouldn't alter his pizza. "What do you care?" the diner asked. "It's not your pizza, it's mine." Bianco retorted, "You don't pay until the end of the meal. Until then it's mine."

On his pizzas being named by many the best in the country: "I'm not competitive. I hope that era has passed us, especially restaurants pitted against each other; that turns people off to the experience. Then they come in and dissect it instead of enjoying it. Jeffrey Steingarten [*Vogue*'s food critic] told me he was so ready to hate me because he had heard so much about me."

On the role of the pizza maker: "We are the mystery of pizza. It's all flour, water, salt, and some kind of leavening agent. Everything else is about creativity."

On the New York pizza scene: "I left New York for Phoenix because I felt uncomfortable about the food as a competition. If you run a race, maybe you are faster than me. Why do people want to quantify everything?"

On keeping grounded: "I try to be incredibly respectful to everyone as far as keeping my hair down and just keep working. If you like my pizza better, it's better. My opinion is nothing. It's as good as I can ever make it. How good it is is up to everyone else."

On what drives him: "Every time I put something out, I think, God, I hope people connect with this. Pizza has allowed me to talk about things that are really important."

Photograph: Gerald Landy

The United States is experiencing a return to basics. All over the country, there has been a quiet renaissance of simple, artisan pizzas. The movement is currently being led by dedicated pie men such as Chris Bianco of Pizzeria Bianco in Phoenix and Anthony Mangieri of New York's Una Pizza Napoletana. Both men are as stubborn about pizza as their Naples brethren, and they speak about it so reverentially, it's like they're discussing theology. "Anything you do is what you were able to interface with a certain humanity," Bianco told us. (Authors' note: We have no idea what that means.)

Ironically, neither of their pizzerias has the VPN seal. There are currently only eleven U.S. establishments that live up to the Naples group's standards so completely that they have been granted acceptance into the American VPN group founded in 1998: Antica Pizzeria (Marina del Rey, California); Coppola-Niebaum Café (Palo Alto, California); A16 (San Francisco, California); Punch Neapolitan Pizza (St. Paul, Minnesota); Naples 45 and La Pizza Fresca in New York; Regina Margherita (Bellevue, Pennsylvania); Il Pizzaiolo (Mt. Lebanon, Pennsylvania); Tuttabella (Seattle, Washington); Two Amy's (Washington, D.C.); and Il Ritrovo (Sheboygan, Wisconsin).

Anthony Mangieri, owner of New York's Una Pizza Napoletana, slides a pie into the oven

Are these are the eleven best pizzerias in America? Not necessarily. (See page 106 for that list.) Rather, it signifies that each of the above, in addition to making "authentic" Neapolitan pizzas, has paid membership fees to the VPN—a privilege that American pizzerias aren't exactly lining up to claim. In a 2002 Forbes.com article, Michael Frank, a manager at New York's legendary John's Pizzeria, said he hadn't even heard of the VPN. "We're not going to join some club," he said. "You donate $250, and they send you a plaque saying it's New York's best pizza." The fact that John's coal oven alone would disqualify it is beside the point: In America,

Photograph: Philip Lubliner

when you're one of the country's favorite pizzerias, you don't need some guys in Naples to tell you you're good.

THIS PAST SPRING, five thousand attendees and 450 vendors gathered at the Las Vegas Convention Center for the International Pizza Expo.™ For a week, they attended seminars with names like "Pizza Crust Boot Camp" and "You CAN Control the Cost of your Cheese"; others watched competitions for "Freestyle Acrobatic Dough Tossing" and "Largest Dough Stretch." There were impressive keynote speakers, state-of-the-art ovens, and more than one thousand pizza-related exhibits. This subculture of pizza zealots spent five days immersed in the minutest details of their craft. Their goals for the week were fairly straightforward: to seek ideas; show off what they'd learned; and celebrate the rise of their favorite dish. Most of them returned home to their businesses eager to improve things—and to pass on their new knowledge to the rest of us.

And that they do. The State of Pizza is stronger than ever. Around the world, pizza is everywhere at once. It's in storefronts, on billboards, in schools, on the movie screen, in children's books. There's a pack of pizza publications to choose from, and countless pie-crazy Web sites boast huge cult followings. Just Google the word "pizza," and you get 22 million hits, a number that includes everything from simple recipes and history to a site dedicated solely to delivering pizzas to Israeli soldiers on duty. Take a look around: No matter what the Neapolitans believe, in 2005—one hundred years after Gennaro Lombardi opened the first pizzeria in the States—pizza belongs to everyone. ● ● ●

Pizza kitsch in 2005

Photographs: Christopher Lowry

Courtesy of EarthStone Ovens

CHAPTER 5
Rise & Dine

AFTER EATING COUNTLESS PIZZAS and talking to pizzaioli all over the country, we decided the best way to understand pizza was to roll up our sleeves and make it from scratch. So we set out to learn how to transform a mixture of flour, water, yeast, salt, and olive oil into a hand-stretched pizza "skin" ready for action.

The biggest thing we learned: Making pizza is hard. After our first crack at kneading a dough ball (which was an experience similar to scraping gum off the bottom of a shoe) we developed new respect for the people who make it every day. As for toppings, we stuck to the basics—San Marzano tomatoes, fresh buffalo mozzarella, a drizzle of olive oil, a dash of salt—all of which you can get at any grocery store. After a couple of tries, we mastered a few techniques and produced some mighty fine pizza—right in our own kitchens. We're not about to open a pizza parlor, but we are eager to share a whole bunch of information about how to do it at home.

Even if you have never dabbled in pizza making, chances are you already have most of what you need to get started. The basic small equipment includes the usual kitchen suspects: measuring cups and spoons, a dough scraper, mixing bowls, and an instant-read thermometer. On the appliance side, a stand mixer with a dough hook is ideal. A food processor that holds five to six cups of flour will also get the job done—assuming that you are not going to produce pizza for an entire football team.

Numerous types and shapes of aluminum baking pans—from jellyroll pans to cookie sheets—are fine for homemade pizza. Those who want to take it to the next level should consider either a pizza screen (a thin aluminum mesh platter that allows air to circulate beneath the crust) or, even better, a baking stone. For a very small investment (the Superstone Baking Stone by Sassafras is fifteen dollars at Sur La Table), a baking stone produces almost the same effect as the brick-lined oven of your local pizzeria.

If you choose the baking stone route, then a pizza peel (a wooden or metal utensil that resembles an oversized, long-handled ping-pong paddle) will also be in order.

An EarthStone Oven, the ultimate for making authentic pizza at home

ORIGINAL GINO'S PIZZA & SPAGHETTI (Toledo, Ohio) and **METRO PIZZA** (Las Vegas, Nevada) offer pizza-making classes.

Metal peels provide an easier slide from the peel to the stone; but wood ages wonderfully, and burn marks on the paddle become a source of pride. It's a toss-up.

Since traditional dough recipes call for exactly five ingredients, you shouldn't skimp on any of them.

> "You better cut the pizza in 4 pieces because I'm not hungry enough to eat 6."
>
> —former NY Yankees catcher Yogi Berra

flour

Flour offers a broad range of choices. Many consider Caputo 0 0 (zero zero) from Naples the gold standard of pizza flour—especially those who are after a Neapolitan-style crust with its blistered, raised edge and tender, chewy center no thicker than a coin. But it has its drawbacks for the home cook: Despite the fact that Caputo has been milling flour for about 120 years in Naples, it's still hard to find in the States in all but a few specialty stores. (To purchase Caputo flour, visit www.chefswarehouse.com.)

People who can mix and knead very moist dough—difficult for a novice— produce the finest Neapolitan-style crusts. Any moist dough will be somewhat sticky, but, because of the purity of Caputo pizza flour and its fine grind, a properly moist 00 dough is exceedingly soft and tears more easily than a skin made with a higher-gluten-content flour. (Gluten, by the way, is a form of protein that gives the dough its elastic property.) It's okay to use a little bit more flour or less water until you find the level of "wetness" you can manage.

Another way to make Caputo 00 work for you is to cut it with a high-gluten bread flour—say, 75 to 25 percent, respectively. But for a blistered crust and a chewy middle that you can pick up and fold, others swear by 100-percent high-gluten bread flour.

If you want to play it safe, go with all-purpose flour. It's easy to use, the water ratio is less iffy, and once you get the hang of kneading and stretching, you will be very happy with your tried-and-true.

Courtesy of Sassafras Enterprises, Inc.

Courtesy of Ledo Pizzeria; Courtesy of King Arthur Flour

EVERYBODY LOVES PIZZA

A TIP

King Arthur all-purpose flour has the highest protein content of any all-purpose flour, which gives it almost as good a "chew" as high-gluten bread flour.

A NO-NO

If you try to use cake flour or self-rising flours, no self-respecting pizzaiolo will take you seriously.

IN A NUTSHELL

The lower the gluten content of the flour you use, the more supple your crust; the higher the gluten content, the more body and chew.

WORD TO THE WISE

Temperature and humidity affect the flour and water ratio on a day-to-day basis. Don't despair. Even accomplished pizza makers have been known to have a bad day to due to weather conditions. If you stick with it, though, you will develop a feel for the proper smoothness and elasticity of the dough.

water
• • • • • • • • • • • •

Water, as an ingredient, may sound basic—but it can cause some surprising twists and turns in your dough. There are two questions to consider: How much water should you use, and what temperature should it be?

Of course, the recipe will tell you how much water you need, but the exact measurement is something of a moving target. As mentioned earlier, depending on the type of flour you choose and the temperature and humidity in your kitchen, the proper amount of water will fluctuate. If some of the flour fails to incorporate into a ball, you may (judiciously) add a bit more water. If your dough ball is too tacky to knead, you've overwatered. (In which case, put the whole sticky mess out of its misery and start over.)

Ledo Pizzeria's Chris Bell does dough the right way

71

The water-temperature issue is as tied to yeast as peanut butter is to jelly. Pizza dough recipes call for dissolving yeast—most often dry active yeast—in water. Pizza makers have water temperature preferences ranging from 45°F to room temperature up to 110°F. But that's where the debate ends, because in an environment warmer than 120°F, yeast starts to die. Once that happens, your dough is a goner.

COLOMBO'S PIZZA & PASTA

(Bozeman, Montana) makes pizza on rice cakes for patrons who can't tolerate flour.

⊙ **A TIP**
Don't guess and don't stress; use a quick-read thermometer to check your water temperature.

🔅 **REMEMBER**
Mixing the dough, whether by hand or machine, raises the working temperature, so start with a water temperature comfortably under the danger zone of 120°F.

◉ **FOR THE RECORD**
Lesaffre Group, a French company that has been making yeast since 1853, says that the ideal water temperature for dissolving dry active yeast is 100.4° F. We agree.

yeast

Which brings us to the subject of yeast, the ingredient that brings your dough to life. True to form, pizza makers fall into several camps on the subject of yeast. The debate centers mainly around dry active versus fresh yeast.

The case for dry active yeast is practical and persuasive: It is readily available in supermarkets, easy to store, and has a reasonably long shelf life—three to four months. (Lesaffre and Red Star brands are recommended by many professional pizza makers.)

Proponents of fresh yeast claim it adds more *oomph* to the ultimate flavor of the crust, but admit that it's less than ideal for the home cook: It's harder to find, it must be refrigerated, and it has a short shelf life (a few weeks).

⊙ **A TIP**
Always check the expiration date on the yeast package when purchasing— and again when using.

✋ **A NO-NO**
Don't be seduced by rapid-rise yeast. It poops out very quickly, so unless you move fast, it may stop working before you have the dough ready to proof (rise).

salt

Kosher salt is a pure product. It contains no additives, no iodine, and has no other flavor. Case closed.

olive oil

Olive oil is the one pizza ingredient that does not appear in every dough recipe. The New Haven contingency, for instance, avoids the stuff completely (we'll explain shortly). But most pizza makers we talked to use olive oil because the oil protects the skin during the assembly and baking from red-sauce seepage or any other unwanted moisture (read: soggy crust).

Many insist on extra-virgin olive oil. EVOO is the oil extracted from freshly harvested olives when they are brought to the *frantoio* (oil mill) for the first press. After that initial crushing, the leftover olives and pits are put into centrifugal force machines to remove the remaining oil—that's regular olive oil (also called 100 percent olive oil). Extra-virgin olive oil simply has a much more concentrated olive taste. Even though it costs more than "regular" olive oil, there is widespread agreement that EVOO is well worth the splurge. EVOO, with its earthy tones, gives the baked crust a more complex flavor profile, which perfectly complements the tomatoes and basil that grace so many pies. Not to mention that EVOO

Courtesy of EarthStone Ovens

THE HEAT IS ON

If you're *really* hardcore and want as close to the Neapolitan pizza experience as you can emulate, you should look into purchasing an EarthStone wood-fire oven, which looks an awful lot like the ancient cooking chambers still found in Pompeii. Here are 3 reasons why you can rely on EarthStone ovens to turn out perfectly baked pies:

1. They are built with a full-stone interior: floor, walls, dome. The stone lining works to radiate and retain heat, and baking pizza is all about the heat and sealing in the flavor.

2. They are designed to have a spherical shape. The dome shape keeps the heat circulating for an even bake.

3. They use real wood. In Italy, pizza has been cooked for centuries in wood-burning ovens. The embers heat the inside to as hot as 1700°F, so the flavor is instantly seared into the pizza. Total cooking time: 2–3 minutes. For home use, however, wood-burning ovens are best suited to cooking outdoors. If you don't have a backyard and want the advantages of the stone lining and dome shape, all EarthStone ovens also have gas jets. Even without the wood, they bake up crispy-edged, tender/chewy pies.

EarthStone has some heavy hitters on its client list (Nicolas Cage, Sharon Stone, Celine Dion), and, of course, the price is pretty high. There is a broad range of sizes and designs, including models such as the Model 90 ($3,000; not installed) and the 110-PAGW ($10,250; not installed). Check out www.earthstoneovens.com for the lowdown on high-concept pizza ovens at home.

Owner Eddie Garza on the claustro-phobic atmosphere at MAIN STREET PIZZA & PASTA (San Antonio, Texas): "I wouldn't eat at my restaurant. There are too many people here."

also provides needed balance for the gluten content of flour, thereby keeping the dough tender and chewy rather than tough.

Nonetheless, New Haven-style pizza is the envy of so many—without a single drop of oil in its dough. NH pizzaioli favor low-protein flour and a higher water content, which produces a softer, lighter-textured dough (no oil to weigh it down) that does not need oil to protect against possible gluten toughness.

If you, like us, find it easier to handle dough that includes a bit of EVOO, you will quickly discover a host of options on grocery store shelves. It may take a while to learn what you like. For instance, oil produced in Sicily tastes grassy green (great with veggies), whereas Tuscan oil has a slight black peppery flavor (perfect for meat toppings). If you want the olive oil of the pizzerias of Naples, go for the ones that come from Campagna. But whatever you choose, avoid aggressive tasting oils that will overpower the flavors developing in the dough. The oil should work in harmony with everything else.

7 QUESTIONS FOR DAVID GROTTO,
SPOKESPERSON FOR THE AMERICAN DIETETIC ASSOCIATION

Is pizza healthy?
It can be, depending on the ingredients. It's a matter of quality and quantity.

If you ruled the world, what kind of pizza would we all be eating?
The crust would ideally be made with whole grain flour. The next layer would be a good rich tomato sauce with lots of vegetable toppings. And then, lastly, a moderate amount of low-fat mozzarella cheese.

And how much should we eat?
The bottom line is calories. If you eat more than you need to maintain your weight, you're going to gain weight. So, enjoy a couple of slices, and don't make it the sole thing you are eating. I'd like to see a nice big tossed salad with that.

What are the health benefits of pizza?
It does a great job of getting the grains in, especially when whole-grain flour is used. And it's a good source of protein as long as you don't overdo the meat. You get calcium (from the cheese), B vitamins (crust, vegetables, meat), vitamin C (tomato sauce), and a decent amount of iron from the grains.

Are there any other bonuses?
Lycopene is abundantly available in cooked tomato products such as pizza sauce, and research shows that lycopene may play a role in fighting both breast and prostate cancer. We're sure a lot of people don't think about that while they are eating their pizza, but hey, maybe they will now.

What is the least healthy kind of pizza?
The crust would be an oil-drenched deep-dish. The sauce would probably have more oil added to it; the cheese would be full fat—and there would not be a vegetable to be found anywhere, but instead every animal part you can think of.

How often should we eat pizza?
If you go for the responsible end of the spectrum, I don't have any problem with people eating pizza several times a week—but the ingredients you choose may be the downfall. Go veggie.

Courtesy of N.Y.P.D. pizza; Courtesy of Colavita

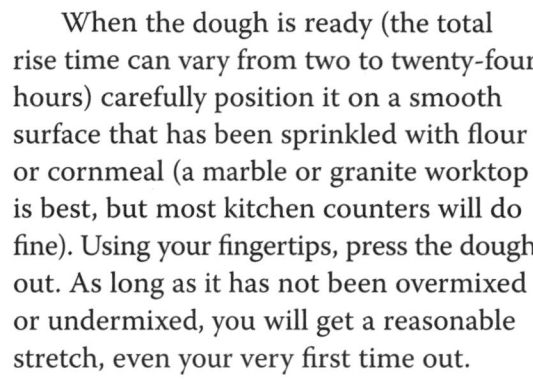

👍 **RECOMMENDATIONS**

Colavita is a good main-stream producer (500 mls: around $9); Capezzana is outstanding, but fairly expensive (a 500-ml bottle runs between $28–32 dollars); you're more likely to find it at Whole Foods Market or in specialty stores than supermarkets.

🔆 **REMEMBER**

The "use by" date on the label is 3 years after the oil went into the bottle, but for optimum flavor, use within the first year.

🔑 **A TIP**

Store the bottle in a cool, dark place.

When the dough is ready (the total rise time can vary from two to twenty-four hours) carefully position it on a smooth surface that has been sprinkled with flour or cornmeal (a marble or granite worktop is best, but most kitchen counters will do fine). Using your fingertips, press the dough out. As long as it has not been overmixed or undermixed, you will get a reasonable stretch, even your very first time out.

Here's a cool trick that will ensure a blistered crust sure to wow your friends (who are bound to be impressed that you made your own pizza anyway): Do not let your fingers touch the rim of the crust (a.k.a. the edge, collar, or crown). Keep working from the center out until you attain the desired size (or a bit larger to allow for shrinkage), but maintain a hands-off, one-half-inch wide perimeter around the edge. This little maneuver will leave air bubbles in the outer rim, which will puff up like magic in the oven and give your pizza the characteristic look of a hand-crafted pie.

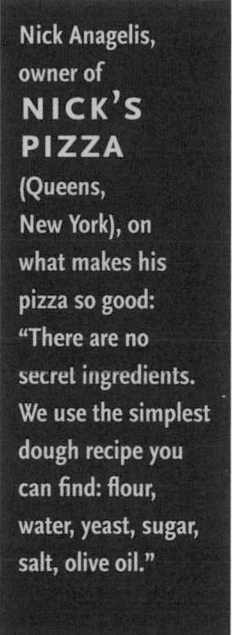

Nick Anagelis, owner of **NICK'S PIZZA** (Queens, New York), on what makes his pizza so good: "There are no secret ingredients. We use the simplest dough recipe you can find: flour, water, yeast, sugar, salt, olive oil."

Once you have your dough ball safely set aside to rise in an oiled bowl (covered with a towel or clear food wrap), you are home free. Well, almost. You still need a plan. Use the time that the dough is on its own to prepare your toppings, flour your work surfaces, and preheat your baking stone and oven. (If you are waiting for a twenty-four-hour rise, get a good night's sleep and do all of that the next day.)

Crust in the making from N.Y.P.D. pizza

But you're not ready for the oven just yet. Stop admiring your hand-stretched skin long enough to transfer it onto a floured pizza peel, which, for the moment, is the staging area for the toppings. The sliced mozzarella goes onto the skin first. That way the cheese will protect the crust from the moisture of the toppings—and the toppings protect the cheese from the oven's intense heat. Then come the drained and mashed San Marzano tomatoes (a twenty-eight-ounce can covers one twelve- to fourteen-inch pizza). Seasonings are your call. A sprinkle of salt can't be wrong; neither can some fresh garlic and basil strips. The final touch is a drizzle of extra-virgin olive oil.

By now your pizza looks beautiful, your salivary glands have kicked in, and your stomach is doing nip-ups. But there's one more obstacle to overcome: getting the pizza off the peel and onto the baking stone. It's a feat similar to pulling a table-cloth out from under a bunch of plates, but not quite as difficult. The pizza should slide freely around the peel (remember, it was floured). Keep the paddle level with the stone and jiggle until the pie starts moving in the right direction. Then with a quick jerk, pull the paddle away and, voilà, the pie will be safely perched on the stone. Conversely, you may run into trouble getting the pie off the stone after baking. Here's a trick that we picked up from pizzatherapy.com: Use a piece of dental floss wider than the pizza and slide it

Above, an N.Y.P.D pizza with tomatoes—one step before adding basil and olive oil; right, pizza utensils from Sassafras

Courtesy of Sassafras Enterprises, Inc.; Courtesy of N.Y.P.D. pizza

Courtesy of Cuisinart

under the dough to loosen it. (If you are using a pizza pan instead of a baking stone, do your stretching and assembling right in a lightly oiled and floured pan, and pop it into the oven.)

Ten to fifteen minutes later (depends on the thickness of your skin and oven temperature), slide the peel under your pizza and remove it from the oven. If you like an extra hit of cheese, now is the time to sprinkle on some Parmesan or Romano. Then let the pie—which by now should be a perfect combination of crispy/chewy crust, slightly brûléed cheese, and tangy tomatoes—sit for a couple of minutes before cutting. That is, if you can stand to wait. The balance and harmony between the toppings and seasonings is crucial— but when they are delivered on a tender, chewy, airy, crispy, bendable crust, it's as though the gods have spoken. ● ● ●

A TIP
Practice the tricky peel-to-stone move with a dishtowel in a cold oven.

TOPPING IT OFF
Just about any brand of San Marzano tomatoes, which are grown near Naples, will be right. The one cautionary note is to check the ingredient panel on the label and avoid a product to which water has been added. You want a fresh tomato flavor with a minimum of moisture content. As for cheese, fresh buffalo mozzarella packed in liquid should be your first choice.

MIXING IT UP

A few hearty souls may want to make their pizza the Old World way—completely by hand—and have no use for these newfangled contraptions that mix the dough for you. It's definitely an option, and the least expensive one out there. But we have to admit: There are some nifty appliances worth looking into.

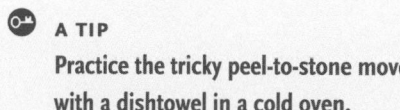

Cuisinart introduced the food processor to the American public in 1973 at the National Housewares Exposition in Chicago, and since then it has become a staple of kitchen equipment. The company's latest innovation is the Prep 11 Plus (model DLC-2011), which features an 11-cup work bowl and a metal dough blade designed for thorough and uniform mixing of ingredients and kneading dough. It comes with a 10-year warranty and can be found at Sur la Table for $200.

Stand mixers are a breeze to use, and there are numerous reliable brands from which to choose (DeLonghi, Sunbeam, and Hamilton Beach, to name a few) but KitchenAid dominates the field. The smallest KitchenAid (model #KSM 150) has a 9-cup capacity and is offered as a tilt head or a bowl lift—strictly personal preference. And, of course, it's outfitted with the key attachment: a dough hook. It also comes with a flat beater and a wire whip, which gives it versatility beyond making pizza dough. A 1-year warranty is included, and it's widely available in department and cooking specialty stores such as Williams-Sonoma, which has this beauty priced at $280 and backs up all electric appliances with a lifetime warranty as long you hang onto your receipt.

Courtesy of Blossom

CHAPTER 6

The Last Frontier: Scratch Recipes

NOW THAT YOU'VE stocked your cupboards with all the right ingredients and perfected your dough-making skills, you're qualified to try your hand at one of the following recipes contributed by some of the country's best pizza makers. From straight-up pepperoni by Mario Batali, to a star-studded creation by Wolfgang Puck, any of these recipes could turn your kitchen into a bona fide pizzeria. (And if you need help along the way, don't worry: Check out www.pizzamaking.com, a Web site "dedicated to the art and science of pizza making.")

Opposite page: Shrimp pizza from Blossom that you can make at home

RECIPE CONTENTS

Barbecue Chicken Pizza

Contributed by Ed LaDou, owner of Caioti Pizza Cafe
Yield: 2 10-inch pizzas

AN EMPIRE WAS BORN in Ed LaDou's fridge. The owner and maverick pizza maker at Caioti Pizza Cafe in Studio City, California, found a bottle of barbecue sauce in his refrigerator in the early eighties and decided to try it on a pizza. "I was trying to Americanize pizza," says LaDou, "and I recognized that barbecue chicken, as a dish, was a real American food concept." LaDou used chicken as his primary topping, substituted the barbecue sauce for tomato sauce, added onion for texture, and settled on smoked Gouda to complement the smoky flavor. He took his recipe to California Pizza Kitchen,

and now some version of his barbecue chicken pizza can be found in pizza parlors across the country.

LaDou's advice for ambitious home cooks: Keep it simple. "Stick with things you know work well together, and don't get too complicated."

The dough

1 tbsp. active dry yeast	1 cup semolina
1/2 cup clover honey	5 tbsp. pure olive oil
1 1/4 tbsp. salt	1/4 cup warm water (108° F)
5 cups all-purpose flour	3 cups lukewarm water (85° F)

① Dissolve yeast in 1/4 cup warm water.

② Dissolve honey and salt in 3 cups lukewarm water.

③ Combine the flour and semolina in a large mixing bowl.

④ Add most of the water that contains the honey and salt to the flour. Keep back a cup or so.

⑤ Mix the wet and dry ingredients until pasty, and then add the olive oil.

⑥ Mix the olive oil into the dough and add any of the remaining water as needed to get a firm, fairly stiff consistency.

Courtesy of Caioti Pizza Cafe

⑦ Finally, add the yeast and knead the dough for 10 minutes. The dough should be smooth and elastic when done. It should be neither tacky nor stiff, but moist and firm.

⑧ Cover the dough with a damp towel or plastic wrap and allow it to rise for about 30 minutes.

⑨ Divide the dough in half and knead it into tight, uniform, individual balls.

⑩ Cover these balls with a damp towel or plastic wrap, and allow them to rest about an hour before making pizzas, or for 30 minutes if you plan on refrigerating them for later. (Always take the dough out of the refrigerator in enough time to let it warm to room temperature.)

⑪ On a floured work surface, flatten each dough ball to size.

⑫ For assembly, move the "skin" to a pizza peel.

. . . .

The topping

6 oz. boneless, skinless chicken breast

7 oz. prepared barbecue sauce (LaDou uses Gayle's Original Sweet 'N' Sassy Barbecue Sauce)

14 oz. shredded part-skim mozzarella

4 tbsp. chopped cilantro

4 oz. thinly sliced red onion

3 oz. shredded smoked Gouda

① Quickly cook off a couple of chicken breasts in your preheating oven. (It's desirable to undercook the chicken because it's going back in the oven for 10 minutes to bake with the pizza.) Slice into thin pieces and marinate in 2 oz. of barbecue sauce. Set aside and chill.

② On a lightly floured surface, stretch out each pizza dough ball to a 10-inch diameter, leaving a raised edge around the circumference of the dough for the crust.

③ Divide the remaining barbecue sauce and spread it evenly over both skins, up to but not over the outside edge.

④ Spread 5 oz. of mozzarella evenly over the barbecue sauce on each pizza.

⑤ Sprinkle the smoked Gouda and the cilantro evenly over both.

⑥ Arrange the chicken pieces over both pizzas.

⑦ Sprinkle the sliced red onion over the chicken.

⑧ Finish by sprinkling the remaining mozzarella over the top.

. . . .

A TIP from Ed LaDou:
Serve this pizza with a Corona beer garnished with a lime wedge, or with a chilled glass of Chardonnay.

The pizza

① Place the baking stone in the oven and preheat to 500° F for 1 hour.

② Slide the pizza off the peel onto the preheated stone and bake at 500° F for about 10 minutes, or until the crust is browned.

③ Serve immediately.

Californian Chicago-style Stuffed Pizza

Contributed by Zach Zachowski and Barbara Gabel, co-owners of Zachary's
Yield: 1 12–14-inch deep-dish pizza (A 12-inch pizza serves 3–4; a 14-inch serves 4–5.)

ZACH ZACHOWSKI AND HIS WIFE AND PARTNER, BARBARA GABEL, lived in Chicago for many years, where they fell in love with deep-dish pizza (and each other). But not the blustery winters: They headed west in 1982. Zachowski, who had worked in several Chicago pizzerias, quickly discovered that there was nothing like this hearty Midwest favorite in California. He adapted what he knew to the California palate—lightening things up a bit by swapping out the heavy, dense sauce for a fresh, chunky tomato mixture and using a bit less oil in the dough. J.P. LaRussa, who has been with Zachary's in Oakland, California, since it opened twenty-two years ago and is now the general manager, has this advice for the home pizza cook who wants to tackle deep-dish: "You can spend an entire day making one pizza. Make it a family affair. A project for a rainy day."

The dough

4–6 cups unbleached all-purpose flour	1 tbsp. sugar
2 cups lukewarm water	1 package active dry yeast
¼ cup vegetable oil	1 12- or 14-inch deep-dish pizza pan

① In a large bowl, dissolve the sugar and the yeast in the water. Let stand until bubbly.

② Stir in the oil.

③ Stir in 4 cups of flour until smooth.

④ Slowly mix in more flour as needed to form a firm dough ball.

⑤ Knead the dough on a lightly floured surface until it's smooth and elastic.

⑥ Lightly grease another bowl and transfer the dough into it. Turn the dough once in the bowl to coat the dough with oil.

⑦ Allow the dough to rise until it doubles in size.

⑧ Punch down the dough and let it rest for another 10 minutes. After resting, the dough is ready to use for pizza.

Courtesy of Zachary's

The sauce

1½ lb. fresh Roma tomatoes, chopped into ½-inch pieces

1 8-oz. can of tomato purée

¼ tsp. salt

6 garlic cloves, minced

1½ tsp. minced fresh oregano

1½ tsp. minced fresh basil

¼ tsp. freshly ground black pepper

olive oil, enough to coat a saucepan

① Heat the olive oil in a large saucepan over medium heat.

② Lightly sauté the garlic in the oil to bring out the garlic flavor (about 2 minutes).

③ Stir in the remaining ingredients.

④ Simmer for 30 minutes.

The stuffing

Fill the bottom crust halfway with your favorite cheeses (Zachary's uses mostly shredded mozzarella), fresh raw veggies (diced or sliced), and/or meats (such as pepperoni, linguiça, uncooked Italian sausage, and ground beef). Have fun with the filling, and don't be afraid to be creative.

The assembly

① On a lightly floured surface, roll two-thirds of the dough into a 16-inch circle.

② Press the dough into a 12- or 14-inch round deep-dish pizza pan, making sure that the dough is pressed against the sides of the pan and that it extends over the rim.

③ Add your favorite cheeses and ingredients to fill the pan roughly halfway.

④ Roll the remaining dough to form another 16-inch circle. Place it over the pizza pan and seal the sides of the dough together. Poke several holes through the top layer of dough. Cut off any excess dough near the top rim of the pan.

⑤ Pour the tomato sauce over the top layer of dough. If desired, top with other ingredients, such as fresh pesto sauce or artichoke hearts.

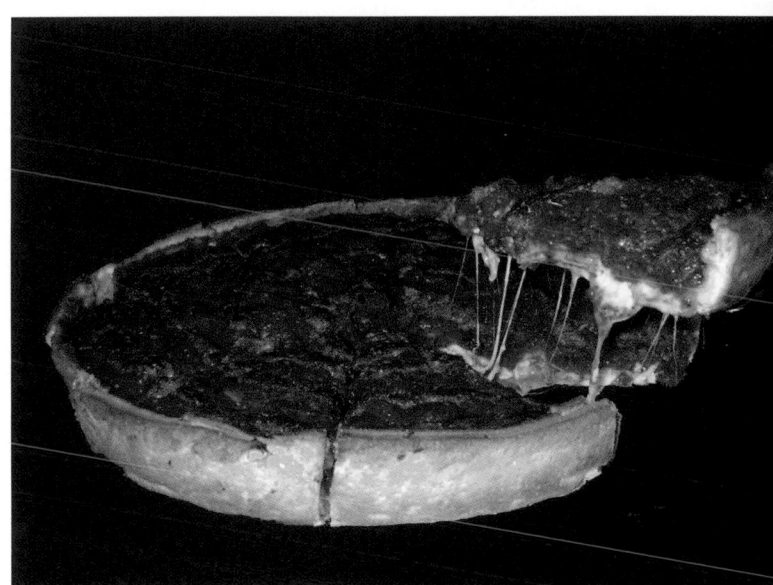

The pizza

① Preheat oven to 475° F.

② Bake at 475° F for 25–30 minutes, or until the crust is golden brown.

Courtesy of Zachary's

Chicago-style Spinach-stuffed Pizza

Contributed by Dan and Linda Bacin, owners of Bacino's
Yield: 1 12-inch stuffed pizza

DAN BACIN'S love affair with pizza started when he was a kid in Chicago. "I used to frequent the original Home Run Inn, and I also made pizza for the family. I started with the old Chef Boyardee packages, and then I would make modifications." He opened Bacino's in 1978, but it wasn't until the mid-1980s that Bacin got turned on to the idea of heart-healthy pizza. "People were having serious conversations about healthy lifestyles, which inevitably led to arguments about whether or not pizza was good for you." Taking a dietician's advice, the Bacins switched to a low-fat cheese, and in 1985 the Chicago Heart Association's Eat Well Guide gave the thumbs up to Bacino's spinach-stuffed pie. And the Bacins clearly got the taste thing right, too. For the past fifteen years, their heart-healthy pie has been the number-one selling pizza at Taste of Chicago, the city's biggest food fest—an event not known to attract anyone the slightest bit interested in anything remotely related to healthy eating.

> When Oprah Winfrey was on jury duty in early 2005, she treated her fellow jurors to several **BACINO'S** pizzas.

The dough

3 cups unbleached flour	2 oz. margarine
¼ oz. cake of fresh yeast	1 cup warm water
½ tsp. salt	4 oz. salad or vegetable oil
½ tsp. sugar	

① In a mixing bowl combine flour, yeast, salt, sugar, margarine, water, and oil. If using a mixer with a dough hook, mix dough until everything is well blended and the dough is forming around the hook.

② Set the dough off to the side in a separate bowl, and cover.

③ Let the dough set for 3–4 hours until it is almost double in size. Do not punch the dough down; just form it into 2 1-lb. balls and lay them on a sheet pan. Refrigerate until ready to use.

Photograph: Larry Lubliner

The stuffing

1 lb. 2% part-skim mozzarella	1/4 tsp. black pepper
8 oz. frozen chopped spinach	1/4 tsp. granulated garlic
1 tbsp. grated Parmesan	pinch of nutmeg
pinch of salt	fresh mushrooms (optional)

① Shred or grate the mozzarella. Set off to the side.

② Thaw the frozen spinach and squeeze all of the moisture out of the spinach.

③ In a large bowl, combine the spinach, salt, black pepper, garlic, nutmeg, and Parmesan. Mix well.

④ Blend in the mozzarella.

⑤ Refrigerate until ready to use.

. . . .

The sauce

3 oz. whole peeled canned tomatoes	1/2 tsp. dry basil
	1/4 tsp. granulated garlic
3 oz. canned Italian pear tomatoes with basil	1/4 tsp. black pepper
	1/4 tsp. salt
2 oz. crushed peeled canned tomatoes in juice	1/2 tsp. sugar
	1 oz. salad or vegetable oil

In a blender or food processor, blend all the ingredients until everything is well mixed but not puréed. (There still should be small bits of tomatoes in the mixture.)

. . . .

> ⊙ **TIPS from Dan Bacin:**
>
> **Do not mix the dough at high speed. This overheats the dough and might cause the yeast to die.**
>
> **Do not place the pizza pan on a sheet tray inside the oven; the bottom of the pizza will burn.**

The assembly

① Butter the bottom and sides of a 2-inch-deep, 12-inch round (or heart-shaped, as pictured here) pizza or pie tin.

② Roll out a 1-lb. ball of pizza dough until it is about 1/8 inch or a little less in thickness.

③ Lay the dough in the pan and work your way around the pan, lightly pressing the dough up the sides and making sure the dough is flat on the bottom of the pan with no bubbles between the dough and the pan.

④ Fill the pan with the spinach mix a little over halfway up the sides of the pan.

⑤ Roll out the other 1-lb. dough ball, but this time roll it thinner than the bottom dough.

⑥ Lay this piece of dough over the top of the pan.

⑦ Tear a little hole in the center of the dough.

⑧ Work your way around the edges of the pizza, pressing the dough firmly to the sides of the pan and the other dough.

⑨ Trim off extra dough so it is even with the top of the pizza pan.

⑩ Spread the sauce on the top of the pizza so it is completely covered; sprinkle a little Parmesan cheese mixed with a little oregano on top if desired.

. . . .

The pizza

① Place a baking stone in the oven and preheat the oven to 375° F. (If you don't have a baking stone, you can bake the pizza right on the oven rack.)

② Place the deep-dish pan on a baking stone (or oven rack). Rotate the pizza a few times so that it bakes evenly, and remember that oven temperatures may vary.

③ Bake for approximately 25–30 minutes, until golden brown and cheese is soft in the center.

Cora Family Pizza

Contributed by Eileen Cora
Yield: 1 11x17-inch pizza

EILEEN CORA, whose husband, John, sells specialty pizza equipment through his Illinois-based company, Cora Imports Ltd., doesn't know exactly where her recipe came from. She learned the technique of making the dough by watching her mother-in-law, Maria Angiolino, a native of Cerignola in southern Italy. "She always made the sign of the cross in the dough before she set it down for raising," says Eileen. "I think she was blessing the bread." Angiolino did everything by hand—a tradition Eileen respects but can't follow to the letter. "Her hands were so strong, she could do anything. I have to use a Cuisinart to mix the dough. But my mother-in-law taught me how to cook—so I could cook for her son."

(I watched Eileen at work in her kitchen in Burr Ridge, Illinois, took these notes, and successfully made Cora Family Pizza—on my second try—for my family. —P.P.)

Photograph: Eileen Cora

The dough

3/4 cup warm water (105° F)
1 package active dry yeast
1 tbsp. sugar (to activate the yeast)
3 cups flour

1 tsp. salt
extra-virgin olive oil, enough to coat your mixing bowl and baking pan
1/4 cup water (room temp.)

① In a glass, mix 3/4 cup water, the yeast, and the sugar.

② Put the glass inside the oven. (Do not turn the oven on; the inside of the oven is warmer than the kitchen. The yeast should grow in less than 10 minutes.)

③ Coat a mixing bowl with olive oil (use a paper towel to minimize the amount of oil—a bare coating will do).

④ Lightly flour a board (for kneading and stretching the dough).

⑤ Prepare a shallow 11-by-17-inch baking pan by drizzling it with olive oil (spread with a paper tower or rubber brush) and then sprinkling it evenly with flour.

⑥ Place the flour, salt, and yeast mixture (when ready) in the food processor.

⑦ Drizzle with 1 circle of olive oil.

⑧ Have the ¼ cup warm water nearby to add if necessary.

⑨ Mix in the processor until the dough ball forms (add water only if needed to form the dough ball). Remove as soon as the dough ball is formed. Do not overmix.

⑩ Knead the dough on the floured board. Form a ball and place it in the oiled bowl.

⑪ Make cross marks with a knife. Drape the bowl with a damp towel (paper or cloth) and place back in the oven (still not turned on). After 30–40 minutes, the dough should be bulging around the knife marks.

⑫ Punch down the dough. Knead again and return to the bowl for a second 30–40-minute rise. (Use this time to prepare the topping.)

⑬ Hand-stretch the dough on the baking pan and place back in the oven to rest for (no more than) 10 minutes. (The dough is "stressed" from being worked on.)

⑭ Bake for 10 minutes at 200° F (a just-warm oven).

⊙ **TIPS from Eileen Cora:**

A Cuisinart food processor holds up to 5½ cups of flour and is large enough to make 1 crust. Unless you are going to make large batches of dough, there's no need to use a dough hook.

Use Red Star active yeast, but always check the expiration date on the package.

The temperature of the water is important; if it's too hot, the yeast won't grow.

The topping

1 28-oz. can of San Marzano plum-shaped tomatoes	fresh buffalo mozzarella (enough slices for 1 layer)
oregano, to taste	salt and pepper, to taste
olive oil, to taste	

① Rinse the sauce off the plum tomatoes, drain well, and mash the whole tomatoes with a fork.

② Sprinkle the mashed tomatoes with oregano.

③ Spread the tomatoes on the lightly baked crust.

④ Cover with sliced mozzarella.

⑤ Season to taste with salt and pepper.

⑥ Drizzle with olive oil.

The pizza

① Preheat oven to 450° F.

② Bake 10 minutes. (You don't want to burn the cheese before the crust is done.)

Modesto Neapolitan-style Pizza

Contributed by John Arena and Sam Facchini, owners of Metro Pizza
Yield: 3 12-inch pizzas

JOHN ARENA AND SAM FACCHINI, partners at Metro Pizza in Las Vegas, are cousins and best friends. They grew up on New York City pizza, and in 1979 they spent some time in Vegas—where they learned that no one knew how to make a decent pizza. So Arena and Facchini stayed in the desert, opened Metro Pizza in 1980, dubbed themselves "The Pizza Guy" and "The Other Pizza Guy," and proceeded to give each customer the pie of his dreams. Refreshingly, neither guy plays favorites; they believe every pizza version has its virtues—and they pack the Metro menu with pizza styles from New Haven to Memphis to Chicago to Modesto. Forget thick and thin, says Arena. "The important thing is that people experience what pizza is supposed to be. It's supposed to come out of an oven, and shared and eaten where it was made."

A chef prepares dough in the Metro Pizza kitchen

The dough

1 cup room-temperature bottled water	3 cups high-gluten bread flour
3 grams fresh yeast, or 1 packet dry active yeast	1 tsp. salt
¼ cup extra-virgin olive oil	extra flour for dusting work surfaces

① In a KitchenAid (or similar) mixer, dissolve the yeast in water and let it stand for 10 minutes.

② Add olive oil and salt to the water and yeast, and mix with the beater attachment for 1 minute.

③ Blend in 1 cup of flour and mix at a slow speed for 2 minutes.

④ Change the mixer to the hook attachment and add the remaining flour.

⑤ Mix for 7 minutes, scraping the sides of the bowl to incorporate all of the flour.

⑥ Dust a smooth, nonporous work surface with flour. Remove the dough from the bowl and knead it by hand until it's smooth and velvety.

⑦ Divide the dough ball into 3 equal pieces, and work each section into a smooth ball by turning the edges toward the center.

Photograph: Marilyn Heckmyer

⑧ Place each dough ball in a separate well-oiled bowl and cover with plastic wrap.

⑨ Let the dough rise in the refrigerator for 24 hours.

⑩ Take the dough out of the refrigerator an hour before you work with it.

⑪ Lightly flour your work surfaces (including the pizza peel) and your dough ball.

⑫ Using your fingertips, press the dough out, leaving a half-inch rim around the edge.

⑬ When the dough is stretched to 14 inches, place it on the peel.

The topping *(for 1 dough ball)*

7 oz. whole-milk mozzarella, sliced ⅙-inch thick

½ cup vine-ripened San Marzano tomatoes

½ tbsp. freshly grated imported Romano cheese

½ tsp. extra-virgin olive oil

fresh Mediterranean oregano

½ cup roasted mushrooms

2 oz. raw bulk Italian sausage

½ tsp. fresh minced garlic

① Place the sliced mozzarella on the pizza dough first.

② Squeeze the excess moisture out of the tomatoes, mash them, and spread them evenly over the cheese.

③ Sprinkle with fresh garlic, Romano cheese, and olive oil.

④ Season with oregano, crushing the fresh leaves between your fingertips as you sprinkle the herb.

⑤ Spread roasted mushrooms across the pie.

⑥ Pinch off small pieces of sausage and distribute them evenly.

The pizza

① Place the baking stone in the oven and preheat to 525° F for 1 hour.

② Slide the pizza off the peel onto the preheated stone and bake at 525° F for about 12 minutes.

TIPS from Arena and Facchini:

For quicker dough, use warm water (100° F), and let the dough rise at room temperature until doubled in bulk.

For a light, airy, and blistered edge, never let your hands compress the rim of the dough.

Photograph: Christopher Lowry

New Haven–style White Pizza
Sautéed Spinach with Cheddar, Mozzarella, and Monterey Jack Cheeses

Contributed by Lou Abate, owner of Abate Apizza & Seafood Restaurant

Yield: 1 12-inch pizza

LOU ABATE belongs to a select group of pizza makers with a Wooster Street address. His restaurant, Abate Apizza, has been on the famous street for thirty-five years, and he's as mystified as the rest of us by the New Haven pizza phenomenon. "People are traveling around the world like pizza hunters and it always leads them back to Wooster Street," he says. "It's the technique, which is very difficult to define."

"Watching Lou make pies is literally like watching Yoda juggle without touching the balls," says Michael Weinstein, an Abate protégé. "When Lou is spreading toppings on pizza, it's like his fingers don't touch the toppings. I have to believe that making pizza, to Lou, is literally like breathing." A generous mentor, Abate shared his crust recipe with Weinstein, who used it to bring a taste of New Haven to the Midwest at Tomatoes Apizza (Farmington Hills, Michigan). And Abate shared his new personal favorite, spinach pie, with us. "People just flip out over this one," he says.

Photograph: Michelle Komie

> "There's a pizza place near where I live that sells only slices. In the back you can see a guy tossing a triangle in the air."
>
> —comedian Steven Wright

The dough

½ tsp. instant dry yeast

⅓ cup water (lukewarm, or room temperature)

⅔ cup all-purpose flour

½ tsp. salt

① Dissolve yeast in water.

② Add flour and salt.

③ Mix at the lowest setting of a stand mixer with a dough hook for 3 minutes, or knead by hand 4–6 minutes (any longer than that causes the gluten to break down).

④ Refrigerate the dough for 4 hours and then let it stand 1 hour at room temperature before you work with it. (The dough will hold in the refrigerator for up to 24 hours.)

⑤ Place the dough ball on a floured work surface and "flatten the dough and stretch it out." For assembly, move the "skin" to a lightly floured pizza peel.

· ·

⊶ TIPS from Lou Abate:

If you overmix, your dough won't rise and your crust will be tough.

Baking on a brick is best, but if one is not available, bake on a screen or a pan.

The topping

¼ cup shredded Cheddar

¼ cup shredded high-fat mozzarella

¼ cup shredded Monterey

3 oz. fresh spinach

fresh chopped garlic, to taste

salt and pepper, to taste

3 oz. fresh ricotta

1 small package of grape tomatoes

pastry tube

olive oil, to taste

① Toss the shredded cheeses together and spread on the pizza crust, leaving a ¼-inch rim from the edge.

② Sauté spinach quickly with a little olive oil, a touch of fresh chopped garlic, and a sprinkle of salt and pepper. Lay the spinach directly over the cheese.

③ Put ricotta in a pastry tube and squeeze out nicely spaced mounds around the pie.

④ Scatter grape tomatoes between the ricotta.

· ·

The pizza

① Place the baking stone in the oven and preheat to 550° F for 1 hour.

② Slide the pizza off the peel onto the preheated stone and bake the pie at 550° F for 11 minutes.

Pepperoni Pizza

Contributed by Mario Batali (chef/owner) and Zachary Allen (chef) of Otto Enoteca Pizzeria
Yield: 4 thin 10-inch pizzas

Courtesy of Otto Enoteca Pizzeria

"THE FIRST PIZZA I ever made in my life was here at Otto," says Zachary Allen, Otto's executive chef. "Mario taught me." That's Mario Batali, the larger-than-life New York City chef who owns Otto, Babbo, Lupa, and four other Gotham showstoppers. But no matter who your teacher is—and no matter how good a student you are, making pizza is always a learning process. "Every day," says Allen, "you have to make slight changes based on the weather and the humidity." With six years of pizza making experience under his belt, Allen feels qualified to chide the rest of us. "Americans see pizza as a vehicle for cheese," he says. "It shouldn't be. Ideally the key is the quality of your crust. Then it should be how well the sauce and the ingredients combine and make a whole product together." And Batali, the master, believes they're getting it right. "Our pepperoni pizza upholds the standard developed by thousands of Neapolitan pizzaioli over at least a hundred years—I hope they would approve unanimously."

The dough

¼ cup white wine	1 tsp. kosher salt
¾ cup warm water (85° F)	1 tbsp. extra-virgin olive oil
1 package active dry yeast	3 cups all-purpose flour
1 tbsp. honey	

① Combine the wine, water, and yeast in a large bowl, and stir until the yeast is dissolved. Add the honey, salt, and olive oil, and mix thoroughly. Add 1 cup of flour to make a wet paste. Then, add and incorporate the remaining flour. (You can use a stand mixer with a dough hook, but Allen does this by hand.)

② Place the dough on a lightly floured board, and knead it for 2–3 minutes.

③ Place the dough in a lightly oiled bowl, and cover it with a towel. Let it rise for 45 minutes. Then, punch it down. Divide the dough into 4 balls, and hand-stretch them to size on a lightly floured surface.

④ Assemble, one at a time, on a lightly floured pizza peel.

The topping

12 oz. puréed San Marzano tomatoes	4 oz. shredded cacio di Roma (cheese) or very young provolone
2 tbsp. extra-virgin olive oil	8 oz. thinly sliced pepperoni or spicy salami
½ tsp. sea salt	
4 oz. shredded mozzarella	

① Mix the puréed tomatoes with olive oil and salt, and spread the mixture on the pizza dough.

② Toss the cheeses together and sprinkle on the tomato sauce.

③ Evenly distribute the pepperoni over the pizza.

The pizza

① Place the baking stone in the oven and preheat to 450° F for 1 hour.

② Slide the pizza off the peel onto the preheated stone, and bake the pie at 450° F for 10–12 minutes.

⚷ **TIPS from Mario Batali and Zachary Allen:**

Stretch the dough in a slightly cool area. A marble or granite counter top is the best work surface for stretching because it keeps the dough cool.

If your kitchen is warmer than normal room temperature (from preheating the oven), cover the dough balls with a towel and put them in the refrigerator for 10 minutes before stretching.

Cacio di Roma (cheese) should be available at your local Whole Foods Market.

Pizza Ai Profumi Sardi
(roasted eggplant mousse with goat cheese, pecorino Sardo, and a drizzle of bitter honey)

Contributed by Efisio Farris (corporate chef/owner) & Francesco Farris (executive chef), from the private collection of Arcodoro and Pomodoro restaurants • Yield: 2 12-inch pizzas

"SARDINIAN PIZZA? There isn't really such a thing," says Efisio Farris, chef and owner of Arcodoro in Houston, Texas. "But we make them Sardinian by using Sardinian ingredients." That means the ingredients of his childhood: special imported goat cheese, pecorino, bottarga (fish roe from white mullet). Farris, who was born on the east coast of Sardinia in a small town called Orosei, came to the States in 1986. By 1988, he had married a girl from Highland Park, Illinois, moved to Houston, and opened an Italian restaurant called Pomodoro. His brother, Francesco (chef of the Dallas location), joined him in 1992, and to accommodate the overflow crowds, they opened the bar pizzeria, Arcodoro.

Efisio Farris would rather cook than talk. "I let the food speak for me," he says. "Pizza was completing and expanding what we were doing. It's part of our life. It's a good gathering . . . a group that wants to just meet and get comfortable. Have a pizza and a beer or maybe a glass of wine."

The dough

1 tbsp. active dry yeast	1 ½ tbsp. salt
1 cup warm water (105° F)	1 ½ tbsp. extra-virgin olive oil
4 cups unbleached all-purpose flour	¼ cup beer

① In a bowl, mix the warm water with the yeast and beer. Let sit for 15 minutes.

② Dissolve the salt into the mixture.

③ In a mixer, add the flour to the yeast mixture and mix well at a slow speed for 5–6 minutes.

④ Incorporate 1 tbsp. of the olive oil and mix for 4 minutes. (The dough should be elastic and not sticky.)

⑤ Shape the dough into 2 balls, and place each ball into a bowl. Brush gently with remaining olive oil. Cover with cellophane and let rise for 1½–2 hours. (You can use this time to prepare the topping.)

⑥ After the dough has risen, place the dough on a greased cookie sheet and flatten it into a 12-inch-round approximately ¼-inch thick.

The topping

1 medium eggplant

salt and pepper, to taste

1 tbsp. extra-virgin olive oil

1 clove fresh garlic, chopped

2 oz. goat cheese

2 oz. pecorino Sardo

1 tbsp. bitter honey
(substitute: single flower honey, not too sweet)

① Roast the eggplant on a baking sheet for 1 hour at 350°. Let cool.

② Cut the eggplant in half and scoop out the pulp. Discard the shell.

③ Season the eggplant with salt and pepper, to taste.

④ Add olive oil and garlic to the eggplant mixture.

⑤ Cook eggplant pulp to the uniform consistency of a mousse in a medium sauté pan.

⑥ Spread the mousse onto the pizza dough.

⑦ Drop the goat cheese at even spaces and sprinkle shavings of pecorino Sardo on the pizza.

The pizza

① Preheat the oven to 350° F.

② Bake 12–14 minutes at 350° F or until desired crispness.

③ Drizzle hot pizza with bitter honey to finish.

④ Slice and serve.

Courtesy of Arcodoro; Photographer: Jeff Myers

Giancarlo Ferrara, executive chef of Arcodoro Houston

Pizza with Smoked Salmon & Caviar

Contributed by Wolfgang Puck, restaurateur (Spago, Chinois, Postrio, et al); Recipe courtesy Wolfgang Puck,
Pizza, Pasta & More! **Random House, 2000**
Yield: 4 8-inch pizzas

WOLFGANG PUCK opened Spago in Beverly Hills in 1982 and introduced the world to what is now known as gourmet pizza. Instead of ordinary sausage, he made his own duck sausage. No garden-variety mushrooms for him, Puck went wild with wild mushrooms as well as sun-dried tomatoes and goat cheese, which seemed positively exotic twenty-five years ago.

And then one night the cooks were in a panic because they had run out of brioche for the smoked salmon appetizer. Without missing a beat, Puck said, "Cook the pizza dough with a little olive oil and put some thinly sliced red onion on top." The year was 1983, and that was the first "deconstructed" salmon pizza. It wasn't long before Puck perfected his most famous pizza. "It wasn't by accident," he jokes, "it was by necessity."

The dough

1 package active dry or fresh yeast	3 cups all-purpose flour
1 tsp. honey	1 tsp. kosher salt
1 cup warm water (105°–115° F)	1 tbsp. extra-virgin olive oil, plus additional for brushing

① In a small bowl, dissolve the yeast and honey in ¼ cup warm water.

② In a mixer fitted with a dough hook, combine the flour and the salt.

③ Add the oil, the yeast mixture, and the remaining ¾ cup of water to the flour, and mix on low speed until the dough comes cleanly away from the sides of the bowl and clusters around the dough hook (about 5 minutes).

④ Turn the dough out onto a clean work surface and knead it by hand for an additional 2–3 minutes. The dough should be smooth and firm.

⑤ Cover the dough with a clean, damp towel, and let it rise in a warm spot for about 30 minutes. (When ready, the dough will stretch as it is lightly pulled).

⑥ Divide the dough into 4 balls, about 6 oz. each.

Courtesy of Spago

⑦ Work each ball by pulling down the sides and tucking under the bottom of the ball. Repeat 4–5 times to form a smooth, even, firm ball.

⑧ On a smooth, unfloured surface, roll the ball under the palm of your hand until the top of the dough is smooth and firm, about 1 minute.

⑨ Cover the dough with a damp towel and let it rest 15–20 minutes. (At this point, the balls can be wrapped in plastic and refrigerated for up to 2 days, if desired.)

⑩ To prepare each pizza, dip the ball of dough into flour, shake off the excess flour, place the dough on a clean, lightly floured surface, and start to stretch the dough.

⑪ Press down on the center, spreading the dough into an 8-inch circle, with the outer border a little thicker than the inner circle. (If you find this difficult to do, use a small rolling pin to roll out the dough.)

⑫ Lightly brush the inner circle of the dough with oil, and arrange the topping over the inner circle.

· ·

The topping

16 oz. smoked salmon	1 cup sour cream or crème fraîche
¼ cup extra-virgin olive oil	freshly ground pepper, to taste
1 medium red onion, cut into julienne strips	4 heaping tbsp. domestic golden caviar
¼ bunch fresh dill, minced, plus 4 small sprigs for garnish	1 heaping tsp. black caviar

① Cut the salmon into paper-thin slices. Reserve.

② Place the 4 8-inch circles on a lightly floured wooden peel.

③ Brush the center of each pizza to within 1 inch of the edge with olive oil and sprinkle with red onion.

· ·

The pizza

① Place the baking stone in the oven and preheat to 500° F for 30 minutes.

② Using the pizza peel, slide the pizzas onto the stone and bake 8–12 minutes or until golden brown.

③ Transfer the pizzas to a firm surface or heated dinner plates.

· ·

The finish

① Mix the dill with the sour cream or crème fraîche and freshly ground pepper and spread it evenly on each crust. (Remember to leave a 1-inch border.)

② Divide the salmon and arrange it decoratively over the cream.

③ Place a spoonful of golden caviar in the center of each pizza, then spoon a little of the black caviar into the center of the golden caviar.

④ Cut into slices and serve immediately.

🄾 **TIPS from Wolfgang Puck:**

Cut the pizza with a knife, not a pizza cutter.

This pizza is a perfect appetizer for a cocktail party.

Prosciutto Pear Pizza

Contributed by Jeffrey Moogk, corporate chef of Sammy's Woodfired Pizza
Yield: 2 9-to-10-inch pizzas

THE SIGNATURE DOUGH RECIPE at Sammy's Woodfired Pizza hasn't changed much since the first parlor opened in 1989 in La Jolla, California—but the toppings are another story. Jeffrey Moogk (rhymes with cook), the corporate chef and a partner of the twenty-two-outlet chain, believes that pizza is the perfect food for experimentation. "Any flavor that you think blends together, you can make into a pizza," he says. Just don't "overadulterate" your pizza.

After bombing with a creation that included mozzarella, Romano, and feta followed by roasted garlic, sliced fingerling potatoes, Kalamata olives, diced tomatoes, and a sprinkling of rosemary ("Everyone was afraid of it."), Moogk recouped with a prosciutto pear pizza. This one didn't catch on either, but once it was removed from the menu, the complaints rolled in. The pizza was reinstated—and now it's a Sammy's staple.

The dough

2 ¼ cups unbleached, all-purpose white flour (If semolina and high-gluten flour are available, use ½ and ½ for a crispier dough, but all-purpose flour is fine.)

½ tsp. salt

2 tbsp. olive oil

1 package active dry yeast

¾ cup warm water (75°–80° F)

1 ½ tbsp. honey

① Add honey to ¼ cup warm water. Dissolve 1 package of yeast in the water, and set it aside for at least 5 minutes. The yeast will become frothy during this time.

② Sift the flour into a large mixing bowl with the salt. Make a depression in the middle of the flour, and add the olive oil and the remaining ½ cup of warm water. When the yeast mixture has risen for 5 minutes, add it to the flour mixture.

③ Dust the surface on which you will be kneading the dough with flour. Mix all ingredients in the bowl with your hands, gather them together, and place them on the floured board. Knead the dough for 8–10 minutes. Do this by pushing part of it away from you with the heel of one hand and folding it back toward you. Repeat with the heel of the other hand. Then rotate the dough and repeat. If the mixture is too wet or sticky, add more flour to the board (it will become incorporated into the dough). Eventually, the dough will become elastic and stay together in a cohesive ball.

④ Rub a clean bowl with olive oil and place the kneaded dough in it. Moisten the top of the dough with oil as well. Place a dishtowel over the bowl and put it in a warm, draft-free place to rise. (Use this time to prepare the topping.)

⑤ When the dough has risen for 1½ hours, remove it and place it on the floured board (if you are a beginner, it may be easier for you to sprinkle the board with semolina or cornmeal instead of flour).

⑥ Divide the dough immediately into 2 equal balls and hand-stretch each to size. For assembly, move each "skin" onto a lightly floured pizza peel.

Courtesy of Sammy's Woodfired Pizza

The topping

Small amount of chili oil (just enough to brush the pizza crust)

2 cups grated mozzarella

3 oz. prosciutto

12 pear slices

½ cup Gorgonzola

3 cups arugula, dressed with 2 tbsp. balsamic dressing

Apply the toppings evenly to both pizzas in the order listed above, but set the arugula mixture aside until after the pizza is baked.

The pizza

① Place the baking stone in the oven and preheat to 500° F for 1 hour.

② Slide the pizza off the peel onto the preheated stone and bake at 500° F for approximately 10 minutes.

③ When the pizza comes out of the oven, cut it into wedges.

④ Arrange the arugula in the center of the pizza. "By putting the cold arugula on the sliced hot pizza, you have a nice hot and cold thing going on," says Moogk.

Rosemary Red Onion Pizza

Contributed by Art Smith, cookbook author and personal chef
Yield: 1 11x17-inch pizza

SINCE HIS CAREER BEGAN IN THE EIGHTIES, Art Smith has been the chef on yachts and luxury trains, for a governor (Bob Graham, now a U.S. senator), for *Martha Stewart Living,* and, during the past seven years, for the most powerful woman in America: Oprah Winfrey. "I always enjoyed jobs that were not your average cooking jobs," Smith says. "My whole career has been serving as a personal chef, and the ability to create wonderful pizza and breads like these in a moment's notice is what separates the fine chefs from the average. This great simple pizza becomes a wonderful part of a beautiful antipasto arrangement, or on a kitchen buffet. I have served this time and time again to many famous people, including my beloved boss, Oprah Winfrey. Just remember something as wonderful as this simple pizza made with your hands says, 'I love you!' Here's to sharing the love with homemade pizza!"

Photograph: George Burns

The dough

1 cup warm water (105° F)

2 tbsp. honey

1 package quick-rise yeast

¼ cup extra-virgin olive oil

3 cups bread flour, as needed

2 tbsp. chopped rosemary

1 ½ tsp. sea salt

coarse cornmeal,
  just enough to sprinkle
  on baking surface

① Pour ¼ cup of the water into the bowl of a heavy-duty mixer, and stir in the honey.

② Sprinkle the yeast on top and let stand until the yeast softens, about 5 minutes. Stir to dissolve.

③ Stir in the remaining ¾ cup of water and the oil. Using a dough whip (hook), start mixing. Add the salt, the rosemary, and 1 cup of flour at a time and mix until it's completely incorporated. Then add the next cup. You will note as the flour is incorporated, a dough ball will start to form and come away from the bowl. Gradually add the last amount of flour, and turn up the speed of the mixer and mix for 1 minute.

④ Turn the dough out onto a floured work surface. Knead until smooth.

⑤ Place dough in an oiled bowl, and cover it with a cloth; allow it to rise and double in bulk (45 minutes).

⑥ While dough is rising, make the topping.

⑦ Punch dough down after it doubles in bulk.

⑧ Sprinkle coarse cornmeal on the baking sheet or pan, place the dough on the pan, and use your fingers to make indentations in the dough and spread to the pan size.

The topping

3 tbsp. extra-virgin olive oil

3 medium red onions, sliced
  in ¼-inch-thick rounds

½ cup grated Parmesan

sea salt and fresh ground
  pepper, to taste

1 tbsp. coarsely chopped
  fresh rosemary

① Add 1 tbsp. oil to sauté pan and heat to medium.

② Add onion slices and cook until golden brown.

③ Season with salt and pepper, and allow to cool.

④ Sprinkle cooked onions all over pizza.

⑤ Sprinkle the pizza with the chopped rosemary and Parmesan cheese, then drizzle with remaining olive oil.

⑥ Optional: Sprinkle with additional fresh ground pepper.

The pizza

① Preheat oven to 400° F.

② Bake pizza at 400° F for 30 minutes (until the crust is golden and crisp).

③ Remove from the oven and serve immediately, or allow the pizza to cool on a rack and then serve at room temperature with antipasto.

Shrimp Pizza
(with tasso ham, goat cheese, spinach, & a spicy orange reduction)

Contributed by Aaron Siegel, executive chef of Blossom
Yield: 4 thin-crusted 9-inch pizzas

AARON SIEGEL, a cooking school grad and executive chef at Blossom in Charleston, South Carolina, approaches pizza more cerebrally than most. His inspiration for toppings starts with the main ingredient, the protein, and then he brainstorms ideas for what will best accent that. When he's working on a new creation, such as shrimp pizza with tasso ham, specials begin showing up on the menu at Blossom, and he "changes it up a little" as he goes—until it's just right. "Pizza has been through the ringer as far as recipes and influence across the country," Siegel says. "You can put caviar on there and go as far as you want."

The dough

1 package active dry yeast	3 cups all-purpose flour
2 tsp. honey	1 tsp. kosher salt
1 cup warm water (110° F)	1 tbsp. olive oil

① Place the yeast, honey, and ¼ cup of the warm water in a bowl.

② Combine the flour and salt in the bowl of a mixer.

③ Add the oil, the yeast-honey mixture, and the remaining ³/₄ cup of warm water.

④ Using the dough hook, mix on low speed until the mixture comes cleanly away from the bowl and adheres to the dough hook. (This takes approximately 4–6 minutes.)

⑤ Place the dough onto a lightly floured surface and knead by hand for 2–3 minutes.

⑥ Place the dough in a bowl, cover it with a moist towel, and set it in a warm area of the kitchen. Allow 30–40 minutes for the dough to rise. (It should almost double in size and be somewhat stretchy and elastic.)

Courtesy of Blossom

⑦ Divide the dough into 4 equal portions (or 2 portions, if bigger pizzas are desired), and work each portion into a smooth ball by pulling the dough down around the sides and tucking it up under the dough ball. You can also cup your hand over the dough ball and make firm circular motions on a clean surface to obtain a smooth ball.

⑧ Lightly flour the dough portions and set them on a floured sheet pan.

⑨ Sprinkle with additional flour and cover loosely with plastic wrap.

⑩ Let the dough rest for 20 minutes before making the pizzas (or if you prefer, the dough can be refrigerated and kept for up to 2 days).

⑪ When you're ready to assemble the pizzas, roll out each dough ball to a 10-inch diameter with a rolling pin and flour to avoid sticking.

The topping

3/4 lb. medium shrimp
1/2 cup goat cheese
1/2 cup tasso ham, sliced thin
1/2 cup spinach, fresh
1 red onion, sliced thin
4 1/2 cups mozzarella, shredded
1 cup ricotta

1/2 bunch basil, chopped
1/2 bunch basil, whole
1/2 bunch oregano, chopped
salt and pepper, to taste
24 oz. orange juice, fresh
1 tbsp. chili paste
1/4 cup brown sugar

① Cook shrimp in salted boiling water for 2–3 minutes. When the shrimp is cooked but still tender, shock it in ice water and strain.

② Reserve shrimp and chill.

③ Mix ricotta, chopped basil, and oregano until smooth.

④ Add salt and pepper, to taste.

⑤ Reserve the cheese mixture and chill.

⑥ Combine orange juice, reserved whole basil, chili paste, and brown sugar in a saucepan.

⑦ Reduce the mixture until a syrup consistency is achieved.

⑧ Strain the reduction; discard the whole basil.

⑨ Reserve the reduction at room temperature.

⑩ Spread ricotta mixture evenly onto the dough.

⑪ Divide spinach, shrimp, red onion, and tasso ham between each dough skin and top with mozzarella.

The pizza

① Preheat oven to 425° F.

② Place pizzas on pizza tins or sheet pans and bake at 425° F, until dough is crisp and cheese begins to turn golden brown (approximately 20–25 minutes).

③ Remove pizzas from oven and cool slightly.

④ Top pizzas with goat cheese and drizzle with orange reduction.

Veggie Pesto Pizza

Contributed by Steve Brieske, co-owner of Merlin's Gourmet Pizza

Yield: 4 thin-crusted 11-inch pizzas (each serves 1–2 people)

STEVE BRIESKE, who grew up in the Chicago area eating deep-dish, is the chef and co-owner of Merlin's, a place renowned for its gourmet pizzas in Aspen, Colorado. "I never thought I would burn out on the deep-dish pizzas," says Brieske, "but when I moved to Boston in the nineties, I got introduced to the real thin and crispy style of pizza." After working in Pizza Huts and mom-and-pop places in Massachusetts and Colorado, Brieske decided to try his own hand at pizza. When he and his wife fell in love with Aspen on a vacation, the die was cast. In addition to pizza, Brieske has one other food addiction: He has a peanut butter and jelly sandwich every day for lunch. "Maybe some day," he says, "I'll make peanut butter and jelly pizza."

The dough

2 cups all-purpose flour, and a little extra for your work surface	1 tsp. kosher salt
	1 tsp. sugar
	1 tsp. vegetable oil
1 tsp. fresh yeast	1 cup lukewarm water

① Pour the warm water into a mixing bowl and add the salt, sugar, yeast, and oil.

② Mix until the yeast is in solution (3–5 minutes).

③ Add the flour and mix with a dough hook for 8–10 minutes.

④ Remove the dough from the bowl and flatten it into an 8-inch disk.

⑤ Cut the dough into 4 equal quarters. Roll the pieces into dough balls, and cover them with a damp cloth.

⑥ Let stand at room temp for 1–2 hours.

⑦ Take a dough ball and sprinkle 1 tbsp. of flour over the ball (also spread a little flour underneath). Then, using your

Courtesy of Merlin's Gourmet Pizza

fingers, press into the ball and begin to flatten it until it is 4–5 inches in diameter.

⑧ With a rolling pin, continue to spread the dough until it is approximately 11 inches in diameter. (Use flour if the dough is sticking to the pin).

⑨ Assemble, one at a time, on a lightly floured pizza peel.

....

The sauce

2 cups sun-dried tomatoes	4 cloves minced garlic
4 tbsp. pine nuts	salt and pepper, to taste
2 tbsp. grated Parmesan	3/4 cup 80/20 vegetable-olive oil blend
1/4 cup walnuts	

① Soak the sun-dried tomatoes in hot water for 10–12 minutes, then strain.

② Mix all of the ingredients except for the oil, place them on a cutting board, and finely dice them.

③ In a small cup or bowl, add the diced ingredients with the oil and mix. Or use a mini Cuisinart to purée all the ingredients at once. (Either way, the final sauce should be slightly sweet.)

④ Spread the sauce onto the dough. Make sure to keep the sauce at least 1 inch from the edge of the dough.

....

The topping

12 oz. low-moisture part-skim mozzarella	4 oz. black olives
8 oz. canned artichoke hearts	8 oz. feta
4 oz. sun-dried tomatoes	2 oz. Asiago (1/2 oz. finely sprinkled over each pizza)

Place 1/4 of each topping on the sauce, in the order that they appear, onto each dough skin.

....

The pizza

① Place the baking stone in the oven and preheat to 500° F for 2 hours.

② Slide each pizza off the peel onto the preheated stone and bake at 500° F for 5–7 minutes until the desired crispness is achieved.

③ Allow to cool 1–2 minutes; cut and serve.

A TIP from Steve Brieske:

For a crispy cracker crust, brush some oil blend around the top perimeter of the pizza, making sure that you don't get any oil over the sides of the pizza (or it will be a mess trying to get the pizza off of the peel and onto the pizza stone).

TOP 10: THE BEST PIZZERIAS IN AMERICA

NO. 1 UNA PIZZA NAPOLETANA
(NEW YORK, NEW YORK) EST. 1996

Anthony W. Mangieri makes 4 pizzas: marinara, Margherita, bianca, filetti—and when the dough runs out, he's done for the night. This guy is serious, he's focused, and he makes the best pizza in the country: The San Marzano tomatoes are in sweet harmony with a subtle layer of buffalo mozzarella, while the fresh basil, glistening extra virgin olive oil, and dash of sea salt prime your senses for the moment you bite into the tender-chewy blistered crust. The entire pizza-eating world calls that a pizza Margherita. In Mangieri's hands, we call it bliss. (Open Thursday through Sunday nights.)

NO. 2 DELORENZO'S TOMATO PIES
(TRENTON, NEW JERSEY) EST. 1936

New Jersey's pizza history is nearly as rich as New York's, and DeLorenzo's rules the Garden State—but not with an iron fork. In fact, the Amico family's forks bend like corrugated straws if you use them to cut your pizza. So don't. Just pick up that first slice of tomato pie, savor the healthy blanket of cheese, and marvel at the thin crust that bends but won't break.

NO. 3 PIZZERIA BIANCO
(PHOENIX, ARIZONA) EST. 1994

Rain or shine, people stand in line for hours to taste Chris Bianco's tribute to Naples, a marriage of "tradition, influence, and integrity." Have a "Wiseguy" topped with wood roasted-onion, house-smoked mozzarella, and fennel sausage, and you'll get what he means. Consider ordering 1 more pie than sounds reasonable, because when you're done, you can't order more. (Closed for 3 weeks at end of August/beginning of September.)

Photograph: Philip Lubliner

Photograph: Steve Pollack

Photograph: Gerald Landy

№ 4 PIZANO'S
(CHICAGO, ILLINOIS) EST. 1997

Amongst Chicago's heavy hitters, Pizano's often flies in under the radar. But the addictive pizza—a cheesy blanket, sweet tomato sauce, and juicy sausage chunks on a pastrylike thick (yet delicate) crust—is like deep-dish without the heft. And it's got a good pedigree, owned by Rudy Malnati Jr., based on a recipe by Rudy Malnati Sr., Pizzeria Uno's original bartender. The recipe is such a secret that Rudy Sr.'s widow, Donna, makes the dough in the basement, and the guys who work the kitchen bring up the trays with the dough balls.

Above: Pizza from Punch; below: Wells Bros. pizza maker at work

№ 5 PUNCH NEAPOLITAN PIZZA
(ST. PAUL, MINNESOTA) EST. 1996

Apart from its unlikely location, everything about Punch screams "credibility": VPN membership, colorful Pulcinella masks on the wall, an owner (John Soranno) who grew up in Naples, and gorgeous pies from a wood-fired oven. The staff, which wears Italian football jerseys, serves blackened-edged, charred-bubbled pizzas with a perfect mix of mozzarella di bufala and crushed San Marzano tomatoes. For 50¢ extra, you can order it "wet"—extra tomatoes and olive oil—in the true Neapolitan style.

№ 6 WELLS BROTHERS ITALIAN RESTAURANT
(RACINE, WISCONSIN) EST. 1921 *(started carrying pizza in the 1940s)*

This family restaurant run by Paula Wells Huck and Bill Rivers (pictured right) has defied the odds since the 1940s—no hand-stretched skins here. The raw dough makes at least 2 trips through an old bakery roller, which turns out the thinnest crust and most satisfying crunch imaginable.

Photograph: Jen Ruby

Photograph: Larry Lubiner

№7 SALLY'S APIZZA
(NEW HAVEN, CONNECTICUT) EST. 1938

Sally's was not the first pizza parlor on Wooster Street to master New Haven pizza, but 67 years after Salvatore and Tony Consiglio opened it, it's the best. Sally's widow, Flo, oversees the clique-ish place, and makes sure that every pie that emerges from the legendary coal-burning oven has that amazing, crispy-chewy, almost-burnt, oblong-shaped crust that made New Haven famous.

№8 THE CHEESE BOARD PIZZA COLLECTIVE
(BERKELEY, CALIFORNIA) EST. 1967 *(started carrying pizza in 1985)*

Vegetarian pizza by committee sounds like a really bad idea, but this co-op comes up with a different sourdough pizza every single day. We went nuts for a fresh corn/sweet red pepper pizza, but you might run into cremini mushrooms and baby spinach over fresh asiago, mozzarella, and a sprinkling of roasted pine nuts. Every day is a new revelation.

№9 FRANK PEPE PIZZERIA NAPOLETANA
(NEW HAVEN, CONNECTICUT) EST. 1925

The standard for white clam pizza—the signature of pizza parlors up and down New Haven's legendary Wooster Street—is still at Pepe's. Frank Rosselli, 1 of Pepe's 7 grandchildren, says it's a "secret crust," and that's all he'll say. Whatever: The simple combination of sweet, fat clams on a chewy, almost-burnt crust bonded by a touch of mozzarella and a load of garlic always lives up to its billing.

№10 METRO PIZZA
(LAS VEGAS, NEVADA) EST. 1980

Metro's partners, cousins John Arena and Sam Facchini, are pizza chameleons in the desert. They celebrate the genre by playing no favorites, successfully replicating virtually every pizza style across the country, from New York-style to New Orleans' grilled shrimp toppings to Chicago's spinach-stuffed pies. Their best achievement, though,

is the Modesto, with its irresistible hand-stretched blistered crust perfectly complemented by roasted mushrooms, Roma tomatoes, and garlic.

Photograph: Steve Pollack

Photograph: Marilyn Heckmyer

CELEB SIGHTINGS

Ben Affleck
Joe's Pizza (New York, New York)

Dan Aykroyd
Louisiana Pizza Kitchen (New Orleans, Louisiana)

Matthew Broderick
Pizza Paradiso (Washington, D.C.)

Tom Brokaw and Peter Jennings
Centro (Des Moines, Iowa)

Bill Clinton
Iriana's (Little Rock, Arkansas)

George Clooney
Amerigo (Ridgeland, Mississippi)

Sophia Coppola
East Avenue Pizza (Norwalk, Connecticut)

Melanie Griffith
Rocky's Gourmet Pizza (New Orleans, Louisiana)

Ed Harris
Johnnie's (Malibu, California)

Dustin Hoffman
Lil' Anthony's (Orlando, Florida)

Jay-Z
Anthony's Pizza Cafe (Orlando, Florida)

Angelina Jolie
Pastime Restaurant & Lounge (Baton Rouge, Louisiana)

Stephen King
Pat's Pizza (Orono, Maine) "He eats here all the time," says Bruce Farnsworth, owner. "Has pizza and a Coke. Puts his feet up and reads a book, and everyone leaves him alone. He's even mentioned us in his books."

Queen Latifah
North Beach (San Francisco, California)

David Letterman
Post Corner Pizza (Darien, Connecticut)

Lucy Liu
Arturo's (New York, New York)

John Madden
First & Last Tavern (Hartford, Connecticut)

John Mayer
Fellini's (Atlanta, Georgia)

Luciano Pavarotti
De Lorenzo's (Trenton, New Jersey)

Nolan Ryan
Pizza John's (Essex, Maryland)

Mike Tyson
Pizza Rustica (Miami, Florida)

Courtesy of Marion's

"The perfect lover is one who turns into a pizza at 4:00 a.m."
—sportswriter Charles Pierce

THERE ARE REPORTEDLY more than sixty thousand pizza places in the United States, and who knows how many more restaurants also serve some variation of pizza on their menus? Which means that coming up with the following list was, to put it mildly, brutal.

Granted, this directory is totally subjective, and we're probably going to start some arguments with our choices, but . . . the pizzerias that appear on the following pages are the result of three elements: suggestions from food writers and ordinary pizza maniacs around the country; in some cases, personal visits; and a hell of a lot of research.

We've divided them by states, and included a section on multistate chains at the end. A lot of places serve more than one style (i.e., Neapolitan and Chicago), in which case we've listed the variation(s) the place is best known for. Some of the restaurants have historical significance; others opened last year. But they all have one thing in common: Day in, day out, they produce consistently great pizza.

Alabama

BIRMINGHAM
Cosmos
2012 Magnolia Ave. S. (Pickwick Plaza),
205-930-9971
pizza style: thin crust
This cozy parlor boasts a house special with a pesto base topped with prosciutto, red and yellow peppers, feta, sun-dried tomatoes, and Italian sausage.

Davenport's Pizza Palace
2837 Cahaba Rd., 205-879-8603
pizza style: thin crust
What sets this pizza apart is that it's regular-guy stuff—tangy tomato sauce and fresh mozzarella done in an old-fashioned oven.

GADSDEN
Mater's Pizza & Pasta Emporium
329 Locust St., 256-547-2556
www.materspizza.com
pizza style: Chicago, Sicilian

Mater's "Better Boy" loads up with 4 meats and 4 veggies, but the secret is the cheese: a blend of mozzarella, provolone, and Cheddar.

MOBILE
Picklefish
251 Dauphin St., 251-434-0000
(+1 other location)
pizza style: New York
Downtown, late-night pizzeria offering buffalo chicken and bacon cheeseburger pies—plus something called "The Big Pig." ("The cops order it more than anybody," says owner Mead Miller.)

Alaska

ANCHORAGE
Jewel Lake Pizza & Tea Garden
9150 Jewel Lake Rd., 907-243-1175
pizza style: thin crust
Mongolian beef pizza sounds strange, but it has a dynamite reputation. Too scary?

Order kung pao chicken from the Chinese side of the menu.

Moose's Tooth Pub and Pizzeria
3300 Old Seward Hwy., 907-258-2537
pizza style: thick, thin, and whole-wheat crusts
Hipsters and lawyers alike wait 30–60 minutes for a table at "the busiest no-reservations-taken pizzeria in the country," says the owner, Rod Hancock. Blackened halibut is the signature.

BARROW
Arctic Pizza
125 Upper Apayauk St., 907-852-4222
pizza style: thick and thin crusts
The view of the Arctic Ocean from this 90-seat gem is so beautiful that the pepperoni pizza doesn't have to be as good as it is.

BETHEL
Brother's Pizza & Subs
1725 State Hwy., 907-543-3553
pizza style: "hand-tossed" Chicago
The only way to get here is by plane, but that

gives you time to gear up for the $10 all-you-can-eat pizza lunch, complete with a view of the mountains.

JUNEAU
Bullwinkle's Pizza Parlor
318 Willoughby Ave., 907-463-5252
(+1 other location)
pizza style: "cracker-crust thin"
"Bullwinkle's Deluxe" piles it all on: salami, pepperoni, onions, mushrooms, olives, green peppers, sausage, and hamburger. You can work it off at the arcade upstairs.

Arizona

PHOENIX
Jerry Tucci's Brick Oven Pizzeria
4602 E. Cactus, 602-996-1023
www.jerrytuccis.com
pizza style: New York
This casual bistro lays claim to the first buffalo-chicken pizza, cooked in a wood-fired brick oven.

Joe's New York Pizza
7321 E. Shoeman Ln., 480-947-5637
pizza style: Sicilian
The pans are square, and the gold-standard 'za at this simple NYC-style storefront is an 18-inch Neapolitan pie.

Pizzeria Bianco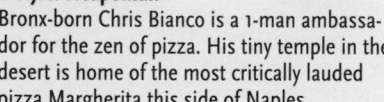
623 E. Adams St., 602-258-8300
pizza style: Neapolitan
Bronx-born Chris Bianco is a 1-man ambassador for the zen of pizza. His tiny temple in the desert is home of the most critically lauded pizza Margherita this side of Naples.

SCOTTSDALE
Pasta Brioni
4416 N. Miller Rd., 480-994-0028
www.pastabrioni.com
pizza style: Neapolitan, New York
The 4-cheese blend of fontina, provolone, Gorgonzola, and mozzarella is the crowd pleaser here, and so are the hunky waiters.

Patsy Grimaldi's Pizzeria
4000 N. Scottsdale Rd., 480-994-1100
(+5 other locations)
www.patsygrimaldis.com
pizza style: New York

Patsy imports the flour, cheese, and perfect ph-level water from New York and has a coal oven.

3 Tomatoes & a Mozzarella
7605 E. Pinnacle Peak Rd., 480-585-6555
(+9 other locations)
www.3tomato.com
pizza style: thin crust
This upscale Tuscan bistro with copper-topped tables is one of the few places in the country gutsy enough to make fig and prosciutto pizza.

SEDONA
Pizza Picazzo
1855 W. Hwy. 89A, 928-282-4140
(+2 other locations)
www.pizzapicazzo.com
pizza style: gourmet
New upscale entry has a nice patio with a fountain and live jazz—and customers choose from 7 sauces, 9 cheeses, and 35 toppings.

TEMPE
Nello's
1806 E. Southern Ave., 480-897-2060
(+3 other locations)
pizza style: Chicago
The place where everybody knows your name and the Popeye pizza has more than spinach: cod, garlic, 2 cheeses, and lemon wedges.

TUCSON
Mama's Famous Pizza & Heros
7965 N. Oracle Rd., 520-297-3993
(+2 other locations)
pizza style: New York
Mama's hand-stretched family-size pizza measures 28 inches across.

Picurro Pizza
1521 N. Wilmot Rd., 520-733-3333
(+5 other locations)

www.picurro.com
pizza style: New York with a California twist
The color of the laminated tables is wasabi green and, from feta to pesto, they have just about every gourmet topping imaginable.

Arkansas

FAYETTEVILLE
Cable Car Pizza
318 N. Campbell Ave., 479-444-7600
pizza style: thin crust
Purists will love the "Purist" with no sauce—just olive oil, fresh tomatoes, garlic, feta, and mozzarella.

Tim's Pizza
21 W. Mountain St., 479-521-5551
(+2 other locations)
pizza style: medium crust
One side is a pizza parlor and the other a microbrewery. The "Meathead" goes down easy with a tall cold one.

HOT SPRINGS
Rod's Pizza Cellar
3350 Central Ave., Scenic Ark. 7; 501-321-2313
www.rodspizzacellar.com
pizza style: Neapolitan, Sicilian, designer
Spaghetti pizza tops the list of the designer series at Rod's.

LITTLE ROCK
Boscos
500 President Clinton Ave., 501-907-1881
www.boscosbeer.com
pizza style: thin crust
House-mixed chile paste tops the "Diablo" pies at this microbrewery with 9 beers on tap.

Brick Oven Pizza
14000 Cantrell Rd., 501-223-3363
pizza style: thin crust
The sauce is zesty, the crust is crisp, and there's a chicken Margherita pizza on just about every table at this cozy newcomer.

Bruno's Little Italy
315 N. Bowman Rd., 501-224-4700
www.brunoslittleitaly.com
pizza style: New York
Six decades of pizza making with Italian roots gives Bruno's bragging rights to the "Mista"—

the one with sausage, mushrooms, pepperoni, beef, and onions.

Iriana's Pizza
103 W. Markham St., 501-374-3656
pizza style: New York
New York-style aficionados give the nod to Iriana's, where the pies are crusty and the sauce is deep red. Try the "Sweep the Floor" supreme.

Pizza D'Action
2919 W. Markham St., 501-666-5403
pizza style: New York
The oldest parlor in Arkansas is a late-night hang for a PDR (Pizza D Resistance): It's got everything you can think of—plus salami.

U.S. Pizza Company
2814 Kavanaugh Blvd., 501-663-2198
(+6 other locations)
www.uspizzaco.net
pizza style: thin crust
"Dave's Favorite" has spinach, squash, chicken, jalapeños, 3 cheeses, and canned 'matoes. Dave, a former employee, is gone, but now his fave is everyone's fave. (Located in an old gas station; ask for the key for the outside washroom.)

Vino's
923 West 7th St., 501-375-8466
www.vinosbrewpub.com
pizza style: New York
The sausage here is cooked in the house brew: Lazy Boy Stout.

MOUNTAIN VIEW
Tommy's Famous...A Pizzeria
Ark. Hwy. 66 (W. Main St.) at Carpenter
870-269-3278
www.tommysfamous.com
pizza style: Detroit
Small and old-fashioned, Tommy's is a good stop before Blue Grass Square, where there's music every night.

California

ALBANY
Cugini
1556 Solano Ave., 510-558-9000
pizza style: thin crust
Hallowed 10-inch pizzas from a wood-burning oven at a loud neighborhood place owned by 3 brothers: Giuseppe, Gianni, and Michele.

BERKELEY
The Cheese Board Pizza Collective
1512 Shattuck Ave., 510-549-3055
pizza style: sourdough vegetarian

There are 3 tables here but the street fills with pizzaheads willing to sit on the median and chow on the 1-and-only pizza of the day— maybe cremini mushroom.

BEVERLY HILLS
Mulberry Street Pizzeria
347 N. Canon Dr., 310-247-8998
(+2 other locations)
pizza style: "paper" thin crust
This tiny black-and-white-tiled store is a little slice of New York, right down to the daily copy of the *New York Post* kept on the counter.

Spago Beverly Hills
176 N. Canon Dr., 310-385-0880
(+3 other locations)
www.wolfgangpuck.com
pizza style: gourmet
Wolfgang Puck's legendary star magnet is where pizza first became chic, and the restaurant's thin, crispy pies with chi-chi ingredients are still pure gold.

CAPITOLA
Pizza My Heart
209 The Esplanade, 831-475-5714
(+10 other locations)
www.pizzamyheart.com
pizza style: gourmet
Laidback surfer joint with slow-rising dough and even slower-rising patrons. Check out the "Surf & Turf" pizza with baked clams, garlic, and sausage.

CLAYTON
Skipolini's Pizza
1033 Diablo St., 925-672-1111
(+2 other locations)
pizza style: New York
Legend has it that the "Prego" pizza—salami, pepperoni, ham, mushrooms, olives, bell peppers, onions, linguiça, beef, sausage, and extra garlic—induces labor.

DEL MAR
Del Mar Pizza
211 15th St., 858-481-8088

pizza style: New York
A family-style Southern Cal spot where the pizza is straightforward and comforting—a taste of New York near San Diego.

EMERYVILLE
Bucci's
6121 Hollis St., 510-547-4725
www.buccis.com
pizza style: thin crust
White-tablecloth Italian trattoria in the East Bay; signature pie is East Coast-style "Timpone" with house-made Italian sausage.

ENCINITAS
Leucadia Pizzeria
315 S. Coast Hwy. 101, 760-942-2222
(+3 other locations)
www.leucadiapizza.com
pizza style: gourmet
Italian restaurant known for pizzas with unique combos (think rosemary chicken and potato) and a patio with a front-row seat for gorgeous Pacific sunsets.

HERMOSA BEACH
Pedone's Pizza
1332 Hermosa Ave., 310-376-0949
pizza style: New York
Most folks like the pepperoni, mushroom, and sausage combo; everyone likes the beachfront property.

LA JOLLA
Sammy's Woodfired Pizza
702 Pearl St., 858-456-5222
(+12 other locations)
www.sammyspizza.com
pizza style: thin crust
Does a wood-fired oven matter? Fans of Sammy's BBQ chicken pizza sure think so.

LOS ANGELES
Angeli Caffe
7274 Melrose Ave., 323-936-9086
angelicaffe.com
pizza style: Neapolitan
Straightforward California trattoria obsessed with authentic Neapolitan pizza since 1984.

Casa Bianca
1650 Colorado Blvd., 323-256-9617
pizza style: thin crust

Courtesy of Zachary's

Old-fashioned, cash-only family spot with red-checked tablecloths that makes cheese-focused brick-oven pizzas and its own sausage.

Prizzi's Piazza
5923 Franklin Ave., 323-467-0168
pizza style: New York–hybrid

At the epicenter of an artsy Hollywood neighborhood, Prizzi's has no shortage of gourmet toppings for its pies; try the Sicilian deep-dish with a sesame-seed crust.

Village Pizzeria
131 N. Larchmont Blvd., 323-465-5566
pizza style: Neapolitan, Sicilian

Absurdly thin pizza made with impossibly fresh ingredients.

MALIBU
Johnnie's New York Pizza
22333 Pacific Coast Hwy., 310-456-1717
(+1 other location)
pizza style: New York

So deadset on replicating NYC pizza, Johnnie's utilizes its own special water filtration system. The crisp-crusted offerings are right on the mark.

MENLO PARK
Applewood Inn
1001 El Camino Real, 650-324-3486
(+1 other location)
www.applewoodpizza.com
pizza style: gourmet

Inventive combos, such as prawns with red and green peppers, and a German beer list make this a Peninsula favorite.

MOUNTAIN VIEW
Frankie, Johnnie & Luigi Too
939 W. El Camino Real, 650-967-5384
(+2 other locations)
pizza style: New York

Watch pizzaiolo Jose Chavez hand-toss the dough in the open kitchen while waiting for your "Tina's Too Too Much" pie: salami, pepperoni, sausage, mushrooms, onions, bell pepper, linguiça.

NORTH HOLLYWOOD
Joe Peep's New York Pizza
12460 Magnolia Blvd., 818-506-4133
pizza style: New York

The pizza gods have smiled on this greasy, graffiti-covered Valley joint, which proffers a killer "Blue Collar" thin-crust.

OAKLAND
Zachary's
5801 College Ave., 510-655-6385
(+1 other location)
www.zacharys.com
pizza style: Chicago

One of the nation's most popular pizzerias, the pizza-art-filled place is always packed. Pies lean to the chunky, hearty, deep-dish variety.

PASADENA
Tarantino's Pizzeria
784 E. Green St., 626-796-7836
pizza style: New York

Hole-in-the-wall with a communal table and a tight pizza team obsessed with fresh ingredients. Try "Grandma Tony's Special" made with 3 cheeses.

SAN CLEMENTE
Sonny's Pizza & Pasta
429 N. El Camino Real, 949-498-2540
www.sonnyspizza.com
pizza style: thin crust

Under the ivy-covered ceiling or out on the patio, addicts indulge in "Sonny's Roman Orgy" (a supreme brick-oven pizza) at this family-owned spot.

SAN DIEGO
Bronx Pizza
111 Washington St., 619-291-3341
www.bronxpizza.com
pizza style: New York

Tiny shoebox of a place sells more than 1,000 slices a day to displaced New Yorkers who order at the counter and eat outside.

Di Crescenzo's
11625 Duenda Rd., 858-487-2776
pizza style: thin crust

Chicago expat Nick Di Crescenzo cuts his pies into squares at this mom-and-pop storefront, which boasts constant lines out the door.

Filippi's Pizza Grotto
1747 India St., 619-232-5094
(+11 other locations)
www.realcheesepizza.com
pizza style: thick crust

The only way to the cave-like dining room is through the grocery store with all its hanging cheeses and imported goodies—and you can get anything in the market on your pizza.

Hoboken Pizza Cafe
1459 Garnet Ave., 858-270-7766
pizza style: New York

Sinatra and Springsteen stare down from the walls of this after-hours standout where patrons toss back pies with tomato basil and garlic sauce.

SAN FRANCISCO
A16
2355 Chestnut St., 415-771-2216
www.a16sf.com
pizza style: Neapolitan

Less than a year after this pizza boîte opened, *Bon Appetit* hailed it as one of SF's best. The thin pies bake in a 750° oven for 2 minutes and sport puffy blistered edges.

Goat Hill Pizza
300 Connecticut St., 415-641-1440
(+1 other location)
www.goathill.com
pizza style: gourmet

Hilda the Goat has passed on, but Potrero Hill residents still frequent this comfortable spot on all-you-can-eat Mondays. Brick-oven pizzas, sourdough crust, glorious view.

North Beach Pizza
1499 Grant Ave., 415-433-2444
(+4 other locations)
www.northbeachpizza.com
pizza style: gourmet

The doughy-crusted pies (such as a clam-topped San Fran special) have been winning awards in SF for 2 decades. View of the Bay a great bonus.

Pauline's Pizza
260 Valencia St., 415-552-2050
pizza style: thin crust

"The object of our pizzas is a very delicate layering of flavors on top of a crisp, sweet delicious pastry," says owner Sidney Weinstein. She grows the vegetables for the pies, which are lovingly served in a yellow clapboard house.

Pizzetta 211
211 23rd Ave., 415-379-9880
pizza style: thin crust
Everchanging roster of organic pizzas, such as the "Farmhouse" with a sunnyside-up egg. 4 tables + 4 stools = long waits. Cash only.

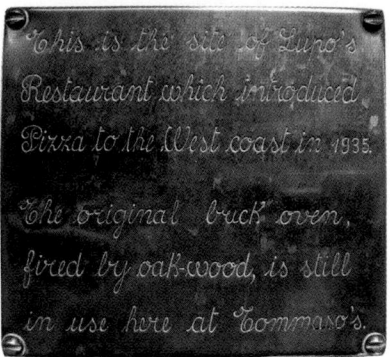

Tommaso's
1042 Kearny St., 415-398-9696
www.tommasosnorthbeach.com
pizza style: Neapolitan
Every time the owners "remodel" the 70-year-old place, they make it look like the same old-fashioned parlor—with the original oak-burning oven to churn out fresh basil/garlic pies.

SAN JOSE
Willow Street Wood-Fired Pizza
1072 Willow St., 408-971-7080
(+2 other locations)
www.willowstreet.com
pizza style: gourmet
With a real chef, an organic slant, and a rotating menu, this place has ambitions. From Thai chicken to artichoke and goat cheese, the pies are topnotch.

SAN MATEO
Amici's East Coast Pizzeria
69 Third Ave., 650-342-9392
pizza style: New York
A snazzy dining room that fills the NYC niche. A basic brick-oven pie is its raison d'être, but toppings run as far afield as bacon and lemon oil.

SANTA CLARA
Pizz'a Chicago
1576 Halford Ave., 408-244-2246
(+4 other locations)
www.pizzachicago.com
pizza style: Chicago
A partner at this popular spot is from Chi-Town, as evidenced by the meat-market "Rush Street Pizza" and a calzone called the "Ditka."

SANTA MONICA
Wildflour Boston Pizza
2807 Main St., 310-392-3300
(+1 other location)
pizza style: Boston (like New York, but smaller)
East Coast thin crust mates with Cal-gourmet to produce pesto-artichoke love child. Enjoy it on the back patio.

SOLANA BEACH
Pizza Port
135 N. Highway 101, 858-481-7332
www.pizzaport.com
pizza style: Chicago
Cheese-on-top pies with whole-grain-beer crust at this surfer-centric brewpub a block from the beach. ("No socks, no shoes, no problem.")

STUDIO CITY
Caioti Pizza Cafe
4346 Tujunga Ave., 818-761-3588
www.caiotipizzacafe.com
pizza style: New York, gourmet
Ed LaDou, the brains behind the famous West Coast pies at Spago and CPK, now runs this humble cafe known for BBQ chicken pizza.

TEMECULA
Temecula Pizza Company
44535 Bedford Ct., 951-694-9463
pizza style: gourmet
Tucked behind a gas station, this movie-themed gem churns out offbeat gourmet pies (i.e., the "Zane Grey" and "Love Potion #9").

VENICE
Abbot's Pizza
1407 Abbot Kinney Blvd., 310-396-7334
pizza style: New York, "but with a California flavor"
Tiny, noisy storefront in the heart of Venice makes 30 different styles of gourmet pizza in a stone-baked oven.

WALNUT CREEK
Tomatina
1325 N. Main St., 925-930-9999
(+2 other locations)
www.tomatina.com
pizza style: "somewhere between New York and California"
A Napa Valley chef opened this stylish spot (note the wine list) to pay homage to a famous Spanish tomato fest. Flatbread pizzas, organic sauce.

WEST HOLLYWOOD
Albano's Brooklyn Pizzeria
7261 Melrose Ave., 323-934-2494
(+1 other location)
pizza style: New York
New Yawk meets Hollywood in a bustling pizzeria serving pies with names like "Yo Vinnie" and "Badda Bing Badda Boom."

Colorado

ASPEN
Merlin's Gourmet Pizza
321 E. Hopkins Ave., 970-544-4644
pizza style: gourmet
A white tablecloth Italian bistro where it's a tossup between the pesto splash and the fresh spinach pie.

BEAVER CREEK
Blue Moose
122 The Plaza, 970-845-8666
pizza style: eclectic
Good ski fuel at this offbeat spot includes the boundary-stretching Bali Pie: roasted chicken, tomatoes, Gouda, and cilantro over a spicy peanut sauce.

BOULDER
Abo's Pizza
1110 13th St., 303-443-3199
(+15 other locations)
www.abosinc.com
pizza style: New York
Opened by a CU dropout who learned Pizza 101 at Rocky Graziano's in New York, this little storefront has been satisfying students with late-night munchies since 1977.

Carelli's of Boulder
645 30th St., 303-938-9300
www.carellis.com

EVERYBODY LOVES PIZZA

Photograph: Steve Pollack

Courtesy of The Sink

pizza style: gourmet

Savor a fantastic wood-fired pizza with jumbo tiger shrimp, Gorgonzola, and scallions from the open fireplace in this eye-popping ristorante.

The Sink
1165 13th St., 303-444-7465
www.thesink.com
pizza style: Colorado ("thin crust, wide edge, heavy toppings")

Raucous, low-ceilinged joint known for "ugly crust pizzas" such as the "Buddha Basil" with tofu and other joys. Its most famous employee, Robert Redford, used to sweep the floors.

DENVER
Carl's Italian Restaurant
3800 W. 38th Ave., 303-477-1694
pizza style: Chicago

Unassuming blue-collar spot that has been churning out hearty stuffed pizzas for 50-plus years. Open late.

Enzo's End
3424 E. Colfax Ave., 303-355-4700
www.enzosend.com
pizza style: Neapolitan

A scruffy little spot whose owner went to Napoli to learn the art. His crackly thin-crust pies prove he learned well.

Pasquini's
1310 S. Broadway, 303-744-0917
(+2 other locations)
www.pasquinis.com
pizza style: New York

Gourmet toppings like artichokes and sun-dried tomatoes can be yours at this hole-in-the-wall fave.

Wazee Supper Club
1600 15th St., 303-623-9518
www.wazeesupperclub.com
pizza style: thin crust

An art deco bar, and untrendy, cornmeal crust–enhanced pizzas have made this spot a LoDo legend for 30 years.

GUNNISON
Mario's Pizza & Ristorante
213 W. Tomichi Ave., 970-641-1374
pizza style: Chicago, gourmet

Beloved ski-town ristorante established in 1971 with all kinds of superb pizza options: thin, thick, pesto, and more. And it offers mountain-bike rentals and hot-air-balloon rides.

IDAHO SPRINGS
Beau Jo's
1517 Miner St., 303-567-4376
(+5 other locations)
www.beaujos.com
pizza style: Colorado

This mining-themed behemoth, with its heavy, rolled-edge "Mountain Pie," seats 700 and spans 4 storefronts. Every table has a bottle of honey for the crust.

LONGMONT
Proto's Pizzeria Napoletana
600 South Airport Rd., 303-485-5000
(+3 other locations)
www.protospizza.com
pizza style: Neapolitan

Breezy spot whose owner grew up eating at Frank Pepe's in New Haven and decided to bring true thin crust to the Rockies. An 8,000-lb. oven, imported from Rome, helps.

Connecticut

DARIEN
Post Corner Pizza
847 Post Rd., 203-655-7721
pizza style: thin crust

Soft crust makes perfect sense for PCP's gyro pizza topped with fresh tomato and feta.

DERBY
Roseland Apizza
350 Hawthorne Ave., 203-735-0494
pizza style: Marchegian (a region of Italy north of Rome)

Inside this cinderblock building, vintage photos date back to World War I; the clam casino pizzas, however, are made fresh daily and sell out nightly.

HARTFORD
First & Last Tavern
939 Maple Ave., 860-956-6000
(+2 other locations)
pizza style: Neapolitan

This original hole-in-the-wall expanded to 160 seats but is still rustic—and so is the recipe for white Neapolitan pizza: garlic, sliced tomatoes, mozzarella, and basil.

NEW HAVEN
Abate Apizza & Seafood Restaurant
129 Wooster St., 203-776-4334
(+1 other location)
pizza style: New Haven

Abate holds its own on Wooster Street—no easy task. The owner, Lou, says fresh tomato bianca is best but he recently fell in love with the sautéed spinach pie, too. Maybe it was the garlic, olive oil, and white wine.

Frank Pepe Pizzeria Napoletana
157 Wooster St., 203-865-5762
pizza style: New Haven

The waiting room runs on the honor system and no one gets into the dining room without permission. But once in, a thin crispy-chewy collar of crust circles the promised land: possibly the best white clam pizza ever.

Modern Apizza Place
874 State St., 203-776-5306
modernapizza.com
pizza style: New Haven

When in New Haven, eat white-clam pizza, but Modern's "Seafood Supreme"—paved with crabmeat—is no slouch either.

Sally's Apizza
237 Wooster St., 203-624-5271
pizza style: New Haven

The late pizza legend Salvatore Consiglio said, "If you treat people like you want to be treated, you will be successful." He got that right. People have been lining up for Sally's pies—be it white clam with bacon or good old pepperoni—since 1938.

NEWTON
Carminuccio's
76 S. Main St., 203-364-1133
pizza style: "thin thin" crust

The owners feel bad about the hour wait, but customers love to watch pizzas being thrown right in front of them before ordering a cheese "mootz pie with crust."

NORWALK
East Avenue Pizza – Louie & George's
84 Fort Point. St., 203-853-9955
pizza style: Greek

> White pizza is the house favorite, but Louie Stefanatos, the owner, loves eggplant and pepperoni on his "very crispy, not too thin, not too thick" crust.

Letizia's
666 Main Ave., 203-847-6022
pizza style: Neapolitan

> Grandpa Letizia's grandsons use all his recipes —though we doubt there was "Salad Pizza" in 1937—and make the dough fresh every day.

STAMFORD
Colony Grill
172 Myrtle Ave., 203-359-2184
pizza style: thin crust

> The "Stinger" pie is topped with hot peppers, but the owner is never telling what kinds of peppers he uses.

WEST HARTFORD
Harry's Pizza
1003 Farmington Ave., 860-231-7166
pizza style: Neapolitan

> Chunky tomato sauce and minced garlic abound, but no worries: Everyone gets a free scoop of house-made lemon sorbet.

Luna Pizza
999 Farmington Ave., 860-233-1625
(+6 other locations)
pizza style: New York

> Oak floors and Italian marble tables set a stylish stage for white pizzas topped with salmon or lobster and drizzled with olive oil.

Delaware

GREENVILLE
Pizza By Elizabeths
4019 Kennett Pike, 302-654-4478
www.pizzabyelizabeths.com
pizza style: gourmet

> The décor changes with the seasons at this upscale casual spot that rolls its dough in white cornmeal for an extra layer of texture and flavor.

Pizzas are named after famous Elizabeths— think Taylor, Shue, Montgomery, etc.)

NEWARK
Margherita's Pizza
134 E. Main St., 302-368-4611
pizza style: New York

> UD students consistently crown the pizza at this deep storefront the best in the state. They recommend a slice of white.

NEW CASTLE
Porto-Fino Pizza & Restaurant
730 Ferry Cut Off St., 302-322-3330
pizza style: medium crust

> There's a bready quality to the crust, but it works fine with the amazing amount of cheese topping the pies.

REHOBOTH BEACH
Nicola Pizza
8 North 1st St.; 302-227-6211
www.nicolapizza.com
pizza style: medium crust

> Just in case everyone in this resort town shows up at the same time for an Everything Pizza, this supercasual spot near the beach has 240 seats and 7 ovens.

WILMINGTON
Café Napoli Restaurant & Pizzeria
4391 Kirkwood Hwy., 302-999-7553
pizza style: Neapolitan, Sicilian

> Friendly spot where the thin-crust tomato and broccoli slice was named Delaware's best pizza by the *Wilmington News Journal*.

Ciao's Trolley Pizza & Grill
1600 Delaware Ave., 302-654-5331
(+2 other locations)
pizza style: New York

> This little shop with a few tables puts out classic foldable slices. The crust is chewy, the sauce has a salty snap, and the cheese is in perfect balance.

Pala's Cafe
701 N. Union St., 302-658-2346
pizza style: thick and thin crusts

> It takes guts to put a sign on your building that says "World's Worst Pizza," but the locals love Pala's pies. No house special: Order it however you like it.

Florida

BRANDON
Babe's Pizza
107 N. Kings Ave., 813-689-2282
pizza style: double-decker crust

> People have been known to wait an hour for one of Babe's 11 tables and then wait another hour for a double-decker that—loaded with enough meats and veggies—could weigh in at 10 lbs.

FORT LAUDERDALE
Cafe Europa
726 E. Las Olas Blvd., 954-763-6600
pizza style: Neapolitan

> Breezy—if pricey—bistro with minimalistic thin-crust pizza that relies on fresh parma prosciutto and fine-sliced tomato.

JACKSONVILLE
Al's Pizza
14286 Beach Blvd., 904-223-0991
alspizza.com
pizza style: New York

> The Mayo Clinic is right down the street. Is that why everyone orders "The Deluxe," with extra ground beef and sausage?

MIAMI
Casola's Pizza
2437 SW 17th Ave., 305-858-0090
pizza style: New York

> When the line gets long, the owner passes out small slices to people waiting. A favorite hangout for the local cops.

MIAMI BEACH
Pizza Rustica
863 Washington Ave., 305-674-8244
pizza style: Roman (made in square sheet pans)

> Among the 15 varieties available by the slice, you might find spinach blue cheese or roasted eggplant with goat cheese.

OCOEE
Positano Restaurant & Pizzeria
8995 W. Colonial Dr., 407-291-0602
pizza style: Sicilian, thin crust

> Clams, mussels, and shrimp are sautéed separately before they become the pizza catch of the day: "Fisherman Pie."

ORLANDO

Anthony's Pizza Cafe
100 N. Summerlin Ave., 407-648-0009
(+1 more location)
www.anthonyspizza.com
pizza style: New York

People-watch in the heart of this renaissance 'hood while you tackle the 2-lb.-a-slice double-crust stuffed with every major topping you can think of.

Lil' Anthony's Pizza Restaurant
2612 E. Colonial Dr., 407-898-6565
(+1 more location)
www.lilanthonys.com
pizza style: New York

The "VIP Exclusive" is a stuffed pizza with a mother lode of ingredients between the 2 crusts. Everything but tomato sauce, which comes on the side for dunking.

N.Y.P.D.
373 N. Orange Ave., 407-872-6973
(+2 more locations;
in the process of franchising)
www.nypdpizza.net
pizza style: New York

Lou Perlman and Paul Russo put Orlando on the map as a pizza destination. Despite an entire menu of specialties, N.Y.P.D.'s cheese pie is the most popular—just like in New York.

Georgia

ATLANTA

Everybody's Pizza
1593 N. Decatur Rd. NE, 404-377-7766
www.everybodyspizza.com
pizza style: thick crust

Thick is always in, but Everybody's super-thin pizza crisps have caught on big time. Think ricotta and spinach.

Fellini's Pizza
2809 Peachtree Rd. NE, 404-266-0082
(+4 other locations)
pizza style: New York

Order a cheapo white pizza at this slacker joint owned by Clay Harper (former frontman of a punk band called the Coolies) and take it to the patio.

Fritti
309 N. Highland Ave., 404-880-9559
www.frittirestaurant.com
pizza style: Neapolitan

Hip trattoria in a former garage with an extended list of wood-fired pizza options and a pleasant streetside patio.

Grant Central Pizza & Pasta
451 Cherokee Ave. SE; 404-523-8900
(+1 other location)
pizza style: New York

Service borders on surly, but this beloved neighborhood joint proffers giant pies and slices and great, cheap pasta dishes.

Little Five Points Pizza
422 Seminole Ave. NE, 404-525-2530
pizza style: Sicilian

Nestled amongst eclectic shops, this patchouli-scented storefront draws the dreadlocked, tattooed demographic with loud music and a vast pizza selection.

MACON

Ingleside Village Pizza
2396 Ingleside Ave., 478-750-8488
www.inglesidevillagepizza.com
pizza style: New York

Indie pizza joint covered with news clippings and beer signs. Locals swear by "The Ultimate," a slice holding a ridiculous amount of toppings.

SAVANNAH

Vinnie VanGoGo's Pizzeria
317 West Bryan St., 912-233-6394
www.vinnievangogo.com
pizza style: Neapolitan

Character-filled social hub great for people watching. Students and lawyers mix with bikers and baby strollers, and the thin pizza comes in interesting combos.

Hawaii

HONOLULU

Antonio's New York Pizzeria
4210 Waialae Ave., 808-737-3333
www.antoniosnypizza.com
pizza style: New York

This spot boasts "real pizza made by real Italians." Check out the "Wall Street" (pesto and grilled chicken) and "Central Park Veggie."

Big Kahuna
833 Puuloa Rd., 808-833-5588
pizza style: Chicago

Local takeout favorite with limited seating, but it's a find, particularly for the garlic cheese balls and "Da Sumo Special"—a meat storm of everything from kalua pig to Portuguese sausage.

Emilio's Pizza
1423 Kalakaua Ave., 808-946-4972
pizza style: Chicago

Dark and cozy, this island institution is packed with movie posters and hefty, no-frills deep-dish pies.

Magoo's Pizza
1015 University Ave., 808-949-5381
(+2 other locations)
pizza style: gourmet

Bare-bones open-air bar near U of H. Huge beer list and huge crowds munching on shrimp-scampi-and-capers pizzas.

KAILUA KONA

Kona Brewing Co.
75-5629 Kuakini Hwy., 808-334-2739
(+1 other location)
www.konabrewingco.com
pizza style: gourmet

Only in Hawaii can you eat an andouille and rock shrimp-topped pizza while surrounded by tiki torches on a giant outdoor lanai.

KALAHEO

Brick Oven Pizza
2-2555 Kaumualii Hwy. (Rte. 50), 808-332-8561
pizza style: thin crust

The garlic-and-shrimp pizza here is tops, but the tourists can't resist the pineapple-and-ham combo.

KAPOLEI

Boston's North End Pizza Bakery
92-585 Makakilo Dr., 808-672-5566
(+7 other locations)
pizza style: Boston

No décor to speak of, but there's a diehard following for slices of sturdy East Coast-style pies.

LANAI CITY

Henry Clay's Rotisserie
828 Lanai Ave., 877-665-2624
www.hotellanai.com
pizza style: thin crust

A New Orleans native, Clay hand-makes every pizza at this Cajun-style restaurant in Lanai's oldest hotel.

Idaho

BOISE

Flying Pie Pizzaria
6508 W. Fairview Ave., 208-345-0000
(+1 other location)
www.flyingpie.com
pizza style: gourmet
> Inventive place with sourdough-crust pizza, great beers, plenty of veggie pies (including potato pizza). Tuesday is "Gourmet Night" (all you can eat for $6.25).

Guido's Original New York Style Pizza
235 N. 5th St., 208-345-9011
(+1 other location)
www.guidosdowntown.com
pizza style: New York
> Guido's cheap, proper slices do Boise proud. One customer calls the white pizza with fresh basil and sun-dried tomatoes "a gift of the gods."

Smoky Mountain Pizza & Pasta
1805 W. State St., 208-387-2727
(+8 other locations)
www.smokymountainpizza.com
pizza style: thin crust, Chicago
> Cheerful Idaho chain with throwback décor and a crowd-pleasing menu.

MOSCOW

Gambino's Italian Restaurant
308 W. 6th St., 208-882-4545
pizza style: thick crust
> Raucous UI legend known for ample pizzas and 60-oz. "Fishbowls" of beer.

Illinois

BLOOMINGTON

Lucca Grill
116 E. Market St., 309-828-7521
www.luccagrill.com
pizza style: medium crust
> Classic old-school Midwestern pub/restaurant. The "Baldini" pizza (sausage, pepperoni, ham, and much more) has been a rite of passage since 1936.

Tobin's Pizza
1513 N. Main St., 309-828-0410
www.tobinspizza.com
pizza style: medium crust
> College hangout with walls covered in green shag carpet and Polaroids of happy patrons. Each table sports a bottle of hot sauce.

CHAMPAIGN

Papa Del's Pizza
206 E. Green St., 217-359-7700
pizza style: Chicago
> In the heart of campustown, this deep-dish stalwart is cherished by students, pregnant women, and Bill Clinton, who once got a delivery to Air Force One just before takeoff.

CHICAGO

Amato's
1737 N. Harlem Ave., 773-622-4333
(+3 other locations)
www.amatospizza.com
pizza style: Chicago
> You gotta love a place that plays no favorites in style, has all of 20 seats, and cuts the pizza into squares.

Art of Pizza
3033 N. Ashland Ave., 773-327-5600
pizza style: Chicago
> A spare space in a strip mall that sells deep-dish and stuffed pizza by the slice.

Bacino's
2204 N. Lincoln Ave., 773-472-7400
(+2 other locations)
www.bacinos.com
pizza style: Chicago
> A hefty but heart-healthy stuffed spinach with mushrooms sets this clean, well-run neighborhood favorite apart.

Cafe Luigi
2548 N. Clark St., 773-404-0200
pizza style: New York
> Even New York pizza snobs admit that Luigi's rolls out the real deal, and it's sold by the slice.

Caponies Trattoria
3350 N. Harlem Ave.; 773-804-9024
www.caponiespizza.com
pizza style: thin crust
The giant wood-burning brick oven is the first thing you see when you walk into this

family-friendly spot, where you can watch the cooks work their magic.

Chicago Pizza and Oven Grinder Co.
2121 N. Clark St., 773-248-2570
www.chicagopizzaandovengrinder.com
pizza style: pizza pot pie
> Chubby pot pies at this dark, woody hangout are goopily satisfying—the crust serves as a bowl for the chunky sauce with sausage, onion, green peppers, and mushrooms.

Danny's Pizza
6021 S. Archer Ave., 773-582-3456
pizza style: Chicago
> The owners are so into it, they never use a recipe; regulars love the pies paved with housemade sausage.

Delisi's Pizzeria
5806 N. Western Ave., 773-784-6320
pizza style: Chicago
> Helen Delisi was an Uno's veteran who figured out how to make its famous pie. She opened her neighborhood charmer in the late '70s, and the place still makes pre-franchise Uno's-style pizzas.

Edwardo's
1321 E. 57th St., 773-241-7960
(+10 other locations)
www.edwardos.com
pizza style: stuffed
> This mini-chain started in 1978 and grew thanks to its fresh ingredients, yeasty crusts, and zingy tomato sauce.

Father & Son
2475 N. Milwaukee Ave., 773-252-2620
(+2 other locations)
www.fatherandson.com
pizza style: thin crust
> Tuscan décor sets the mood for these thin and crispy pizzas that Chicagoans have loved since 1947. Making 12,000 deliveries a week from just 3 locations must be a record.

Follia
953 W. Fulton Market, 312-243-2888
pizza style: Neapolitan
> In a hip market district of Chicago, Follia's appetizer pizzas are "simple, clean, and good Neapolitan." Italian-born owner Bruno Abate says, "There is no other pizza."

Gino's East
633 N. Wells St., 312-934-1124
(+ 10 other locations)
www.ginoseast.com
pizza style: Chicago

In 1966, 2 cabbies gave up their taxis and opened the now legendary Gino's East. The graffiti on the walls provides entertainment while waiting for your made-to-order golden-crusted beauty.

Home Run Inn
4254 W. 31st St.; 773-247-9696
(+4 other locations)
www.homeruninn.com
pizza style: thin crust

A South Side thin-pizza institution where Tiffany-style light fixtures and wooden booths beckon families on their way to a Sox game.

Pat's Pizza
2679 N. Lincoln Ave., 773-248-0168
pizza style: thin crust

Since 1949, this place has been hand-rolling the dough for the medium-thin crust that serves as a platform for slightly oily cheese and fennel-studded sausage.

Pequod's
2207 N. Clybourn Ave., 773-327-1512
pizza style: Chicago

Walls with endless photos of rowdy patrons—devotees of the hefty pan pizzas famous for sweet caramelized crust.

Piece
1927 W. North Ave., 773-772-4422
www.piecechicago.com
pizza style: New Haven

Loft-esque brewpub where there are enough pies, brews, and TVs to keep everyone happy.

Pizano's Pizza and Pasta
864 N. State St., 312-751-1766
(+2 other locations)
www.pizanoschicago.com
pizza style: Chicago, medium crust

TOP 10

It's all about the cornmeal-based crust, which tastes almost like pastry and holds the chunky sausage in place.

Pizza D.O.C.
2251 W. Lawrence Ave., 773-784-8777
www.pizza-doc.com
pizza style: Neapolitan

This neighborhood parlor has adopted the D.O.C. concept *(denominazione de orgine controllata*, regarding Italian wine standards) for its wood-burning pizzas.

Pizzeria Due
619 N. Wabash Ave., 312-943-2400
pizza style: Chicago

Located in an old mansion, Due's is a block away from its deep-dish mothership, Uno's (see Chains, page 140). Order at the door so you can claim your table and your pizza about an hour later.

Santullo's Eatery
1943 W. North Ave., 773-227-7960
www.santullos.com
pizza style: New York

The folks here say spinning dough is the only way to go. Centrifugal force results in the even crusts for their massive 22-inch, 6-slice pies.

Tedino's
5335 N. Sheridan Rd., 773-275-8100
pizza style: Chicago

The storefront interior has no personality to speak of, but the cheesy deep-dish pizzas are a perfect example of the genre—especially on half-price Wednesdays.

Vito & Nick's
8433 S. Pulaski Rd., 773-735-2050
(+1 other location)
www.vitoandnick.com
pizza style: thin crust

The family here has been following patriarch Nick Barraco's recipe for cracker-crispy thin crust for 60-plus years.

CRESTWOOD
Louisa's

14025 S. Cicero Ave., 708-371-0950
pizza style: pan

The flaky crust is thin on the bottom and thicker on the sides at this no-frills old-time bar.

DEKALB
Pizza Villa
824 W. Lincoln Hwy., 815-758-8116
www.pizzavilla.com
pizza style: thin crust

A townie place in a college town. Cheese-and-sausage pizza rules since 1956, but you can get taco toppings and veggies, too.

ELMWOOD PARK
Old World Pizza
7230 W. North Ave., 708-456-3000
pizza style: Chicago

The thin-crust BBQ chicken is popular but the deep-dish spinach with onions and fresh garlic is beloved. At lunch, $5 gets you 2 slices and a can of soda.

EVANSTON
Carmen's
1012 Church St., 847-328-0031
(+2 other locations)
pizza style: stuffed

Stuffed pizza fans love Carmen's spinach, veggie, and pesto pies made with a secret blend of 4 cheeses.

Gigio's Pizzeria
1001 Davis St., 847-328-0990
pizza style: New York

Stop by twice and chances are that the owner, Julio Andino, will know your name and invite you downstairs to show you how he makes the stuff.

EVERGREEN PARK
Rosangela's Pizza
2807 W. 95th St., 708-422-2041
pizza style: thin crust

This South Side joint proves that not all

Courtesy of Home Run Inn; T-shirt photograph: Christopher Lowry

Chicagoans live and die by deep-dish. The sauce is sweeter than most; sausage reigns; and George Wendt drops by whenever he's in town.

LANSING
Waldo Cooney's Pizza
3622 Ridge Rd., 708-895-0004
(+5 other locations)
www.waldocooneyspizza.com
pizza style: thin crust
> This 24-year-old South Side tradition upholds Chicago's rep for deep-dish, but arguably the thin crust is even better.

LINCOLNWOOD
Lou Malnati's
6649 N. Lincoln Ave., 847-673-0800
(+21 other locations)
www.loumalnatis.com
pizza style: Chicago
> This local chain was an instant legend when it opened in 1971. Outdated atmosphere gives way to wonderful pies featuring cornmeal crust and a sauce of barely crushed tomatoes.

MATTESON
Nino's Pizza
4630 Lincoln Hwy., 708-747-4210
(+2 other locations)
pizza style: thin crust
> You know a place is good when it's been around for 50-plus years, makes everything from scratch, and other pizza makers rave about it.

Indiana

ELKHART
Volcano Pizza
126 Easy Shopping Pl., 574-295-8606
(+2 other locations)
pizza style: New York
> Even hard-core pizza fanatics rave about Volcano's sausage pies, which are cut into strips, not slices.

HUNTINGBURG
Gaslight Restaurant
328 E. 4th St., 812-683-3669
pizza style: medium crust
> Three generations of Hoosiers have been

getting their money's worth with the heavy pies at this family-run restaurant on a small town's main drag.

INDIANAPOLIS
Bazbeaux Pizza
811 E. Westfield Blvd., 317-255-5711
(+1 other location)
www.bazbeaux.com
pizza style: gourmet
> Eternally chosen Indy's best, Bazbeaux boasts endless toppings, good beer, and a nice deck.

Some Guys Pizza
6235 N. Allisonville Rd., 317-257-1364
(+1 other location)
www.someguyspizza.com
pizza style: gourmet
> Colorful spot that's always packed—and worth the wait for expertly made pies, both traditional and untraditional (Thai, Creole, etc.).

SOUTH BEND
Bruno's
2610 Prairie Ave., 574-288-3320
(+ 5 other locations)
www.brunospizza.com
pizza style: thick and thin crusts
> Quintessential college-town pizzeria. Celebrating a Notre Dame win with a Bruno's thin-crust has been a South Bend tradition since the mid-'70s.

TERRE HAUTE
Maurizio's Pizza
2940 Wabash Ave., 812-232-0633
(+ 1 other location)
www.mauriziospizza.verizonsupersite.com
pizza style: Sicilian, thin crust
> Maurizio's makes its own sausage, which they often put on the hulking 20-inch "747 Pizza" named after the jumbo jet.

Iowa

AMES
Great Plains Sauce and Dough Co.
129 Main St., 515-232-4263
www.greatplainspizza.com
pizza style: Denver ("a thick, wheat crust")
> GP is dark and crowded, and feels like a horse stable, but the robust pies are famous for their twisted whole-wheat that ISU students smear with honey.

DES MOINES
Big Tomato Pizza Co.
2613 Ingersoll Ave., 515-288-7227
pizza style: eclectic
> No-frills place to go for a slice after the bars close. They admit the service is lousy, but they'll put anything on a pizza: peanut butter, celery, whatever.

Centro
1011 Locust St., 515-244-7033
www.centrodesmoines.com
pizza style: New York
> Stylish downtown trattoria in a magnificently restored old building. Coal-fired brick-oven pizza topped with imported San Marzano tomatoes.

Bordenaro's Pizza & Pasta
6108 SW 9th St., 515-287-1607
pizza style: thin crust
> A Des Moines favorite for its spicy sauce and cracker-thin crust. On Wednesdays and Thursdays, a 1-topping large is only $8.

Noah's Ark Restaurant & Lounge
2400 Ingersoll Ave., 515-288-2246
pizza style: thin crust
> Nothing fancy about this classic Italian-American ristorante, but folks have loved their old-fashioned pizza since before anyone knew what the heck "pizza pie" was.

Scornovacca's
1930 SE 14th St., 515-244-5779
www.scornos.com
pizza style: thin crust
> An old-school Italian joint with traditional and oddball pizzas, Scorno's boasts a bocci ball court and drive-through slices for $1.

GRINNELL
Pagliai's
816 5th Ave., 641-236-5331
(+ 3 other locations)
www.pagliais.com
pizza style: thin crust
> Kids and students have had a soft spot for the thin pizza and friendly service at "Pags" since 1957.

IOWA CITY
The Mill Restaurant
120 E. Burlington St., 319-351-9529

www.icmill.com
pizza style: thin crust

> Great music venue famous for "Mexican Pizza" with homemade chorizo and fluted pie crust. Sunday is 2-for-1 pizza night.

Wedge Pizzeria
517 S. Riverside Dr., 319-337-6677
(+ 1 other location)
www.thewedgepizza.com
pizza style: gourmet

> The owners of this spot are so pizza-crazy, they eat their own pies—whimsical options such as "The Wedgetable"—every day.

Kansas

LAWRENCE
Papa Keno's Pizzeria
1035 Massachusetts St., 785-841-7272
(+ 3 other locations)
www.papakenos.com
pizza style: New York

> Typical success story: Jersey boy goes to school in Midwest, sells NY-style slices "as big as your face," gets rich. New wave of students salivates every fall.

Pyramid Pizza
701 W. 9th St., 785-842-3232
(+ 8 other locations)
www.pyramidpizza.com
pizza style: thick crust

> These doughy pies, with their golden braided crust and honey to dip it in, have a loyal following that includes 1 of this book's authors, who used to be a delivery boy back in grad school.

Rudy's Pizzeria
704 Massachusetts St., 785-749-0055
pizza style: St. Louis

> You gotta like a subterranean college-town pizzeria named for the owner's dead dog. You also gotta like $2 slices with spicy red wine sauce.

OVERLAND PARK
Barley's Brewhaus & Restaurant
11924 W. 119th St., 913-663-4099
(+1 other location)
www.barleysbrewhaus.com
pizza style: thin crust

> Hopping strip-mall brewery with 99 beers on

tap and pizza crust so thin you can almost see through it.

WICHITA
Knolla's
3817 W. 13th St. N., 316-942-0344
www.knollas.com
pizza style: Chicago, New York

> At this tiny spot, the kitchen accounts for 90% of the square footage. The thin crust with addictively zingy sauce is Wichita's finest pizza—by far.

Kentucky

LEXINGTON
Joe Bologna's
117 W. Maxwell St., 859-259-0495
www.joebolognas.com
pizza style: medium

> Housed in a former synagogue, Joe B's is on the National Register of Historic Places. Joe is obsessed with balance of sauce and cheese, and serves plenty of 6-inch specialty pizzas at lunch.

Pazzo's Pizza Pub
385 S. Limestone, 859-255-5125
www.pazzospizzapub.com
pizza style: New York

> Pazzo's is a college-town success: near campus, serving serious pizzas and great beers, and providing lots of basketball-blaring TVs. Check out the "Mezzaluna," a pizza-calzone hybrid.

LOUISVILLE
Bearno's Pizza Bowman Field
2900 Taylorsville Rd., 502-458-8605
(+17 other locations)
pizza style: Chicago

> This no-frills spot serves a mean super deep-dish, particularly "Mama Bearno's Special," with sausage, pepperoni, and veggies.

Clifton's Pizza Co.
2230 Frankfort Ave., 502-893-3730
www.cliftonspizza.com
pizza style: thin crust

> The crust is the only thing that's small at this humongous space adorned with bric-a-brac (flags, clocks, Elvis pictures). Live blues/folk almost every night.

Impellizzeri's Pizza
2306 Bardstown Rd., 502-451-7177
pizza style: Chicago

> Everything you need to know about this smoky family-owned place is summed up by the following: $37.99 for an 11-by-13-inch Sicilian pizza with everything on it.

Tony BoomBozz Pizzeria
3334 Frankfort Ave., 502-896-9090
(+2 other locations)
pizza style: gourmet

> Owner Tony Palombino's unique creations have scored big in international competition. Nice inexpensive "pizzettes" at lunch.

Wick's Pizza and Pub
975 Baxter Ave., 502-458-1828
(+3 other locations)
www.wickspizza.com
pizza style: thin crust

> In the heart of the Highlands, this family pub features personal TV sets in booths, a tie-dye-clad staff, and the "Big Wick," an 18-inch pie with everything on it.

PADUCAH
Max's Brick Oven Cafe
112 Market House Sq., 270-575-3473
pizza style: thin crust

> Venerable wood-burning pizzas with roasted vegetables and the like in a charming turn-of-the-century building downtown.

SLADE
Miguel's Pizza & Rock Climbing
1890 Natural Bridge Rd., 606-663-1975
pizza style: eclectic

> Open April–November, Miguel's is the de facto campsite for climbers at Red River Gorge. Miguel grows his own garlic and, reportedly, makes his own pepperoni in the shape of goats.

Louisiana

BATON ROUGE
Pastime Restaurant & Lounge
252 South Blvd., 225-343-5490
pizza style: thin crust

> Better know your LSU sports trivia before setting foot in this memorabilia-covered bar. But if you order the "Boudin"—and don't blink at the jalapeños—you may be able to fake it.

METAIRIE
Tower of Pizza
2104 Veterans Memorial Blvd., 504-833-9373
pizza style: medium crust

Remember the joint in *The Godfather* where Michael Corleone blows the bad guys away? That's what this place looks like.

MONROE
Johnny's Pizza House
3501 Desiard St., 318-343-2222
(+25 other locations)
www.johnnys-pizza.com
pizza style: thick and thin

In 1967, owner Johnny Huntsman borrowed $5,000 and opened what he called "the only link in the world's smallest chain."

NEW ORLEANS
Augie's Tower of Pizza
4428 Downman Rd., 504-246-9948
pizza style: medium crust

Every pizza at this quaint spot is "hand-tossed to perfection," says owner Walter Forchlier, and the toppings are applied with abandon.

Fleur de Lis Cocktail Lounge
5655 Government St., 225-924-2904
pizza style: thin crust

Inside this pink art deco building with the neon sign out front, dine on a rectangular sausage pizza by the light of the beer signs and play 45s on the jukebox.

Louisiana Pizza Kitchen
95 French Market Pl., 504-522-9500
pizza style: gourmet

This modern boîte in the heart of the French Market gives its 8-inch indies regional identity with crawfish, shrimp, and gumbo ya-ya with andouille sausage.

Reginelli's Pizzeria
(+2 other locations)
741 State St., 504-899-1414
www.reginellis.com
pizza style: medium crust

If you groove on garlic-butter sauce, this menu's for you. Four of the 10 special 'zas never heard of tomato sauce.

Rocky's Gourmet Pizza
3222 Magazine St., 504-891-5152
pizza style: thin crust

Antique gewgaws hang from the ceiling, and it's regional gourmet all the way at Rocky's: The muffaletta pizza has sautéed shrimp, crawfish, and onions.

Maine

ORONO
Pat's Pizza
11 Mill St., 207-866-2111
(+12 other locations)
pizza style: thin crust

The neon sign outside says Pat's, but the ever-popular spinach-tomato-feta pizza is called "Bert's"—after the waitress who invented it.

PORTLAND
Anthony's Italian Kitchen
151 Middle St., 207-774-8668
pizza style: medium crust

In 1998, a homemade explosive was found in Anthony's bathroom, but luckily it didn't detonate. Tony Barrasso's pizzas have always been the bomb in Portland.

Portland Pie CO
505 Fore St., 207-772-1231
(+1 other location)
pizza style: gourmet

There are 6 variations of dough here (basil, 6-grain, beer, sun-dried tomato, wheat, and garlic) and 11 specialty pizzas with a spicy sauce.

SOUTH PORTLAND
Ricetta's Brick Oven Pizzeria
29 Western Ave., 207-775-7400
(+1 other location)
www.ricettas.com
pizza style: thin crust

The brick ovens burn 24 hours a day at Ricetta's, and more than 250,000 reliable pizzas come out every year.

YARMOUTH
Romeo's Pizza
438 US Rte. 1, 207-846-1473
(+3 more locations)
www.romeospizza.biz
pizza style: medium

Romeo's Greek owner tops his signature pie with spinach, sausage, feta, and ricotta and calls it "Spanakopita."

Maryland

BALTIMORE
Café Isis/Al Pacino Café
1809 Reisterstown Rd., 410-653-6868
(+2 other locations)
www.cafeisis.com
pizza style: pita-like

Styled to feel like an Egyptian temple, Pacino's turns out pita-style crust from its wood-burning oven. Topping innovations: felafel and tahini.

Egyptian Pizza
542 E. Belvedere Ave., 410-323-7060
(+2 other locations)
www.egyptianpizza.com
pizza style: pita-like

The giant lotus flower and the hieroglyphics are faux, but the "Sharm El-Sheq" (covered with Boursin cheese, smoked salmon, and red and black caviar) put this parlor on the pizza map.

Fortunato Brothers Pizza
6374 York Rd., 410-377-7300
pizza style: New York

At this college-town take-out joint, the chopped-tomato white pizza makes the dean's list every year.

Matthew's Pizzeria
3131 Eastern Ave., 410-276-8755
pizza style: Chicago

The walls of the newly spiffed old row house sport endless pizza awards. The secret is in the hand-cut cheeses and high oven temperature.

ESSEX
Pizza John's
113 Back River Neck Rd., 410-687-7733
www.pizzajohns.com
pizza style: thin crust

Once you see the giant pizza man statue outside, chances are you're gonna stop at this off-the-beaten-track gem.

EVERYBODY LOVES PIZZA

Photograph: Patrick R. Wagner

LAUREL
Pal Jacks Pizza
310 Main St., 301-725-5225
pizza style: thin crust

Admirers of PJ's pastry-style crust drive from miles around to dine in or carry home a piping hot pepperoni or sausage pie.

ROCKVILLE
Siena's Pizzeria
11417 Woodglen Dr., 301-770-7474
pizza style: Chicago, thin crust

Siena's pizzas are strictly vegetarian and kosher. Customers swear the soy sausage tastes like meat.

Massachusetts

AMESBURY
Flatbread Company
5 Market Sq., 978-834-9800
(+2 other locations)
www.flatbreadcompany.com
pizza style: thin crust

At this converted mill, the chicken is free-range, the pepperoni is nitrate-free, and the pizzas have names like "Punctuated Equilibrium."

AMHERST
Antonio's
31 N. Pleasant St., 413-253-0808
(+2 other locations)
www.antoniospizzas.com
pizza style: gourmet

Any kind of slice you want (avocado enchilada, buffalo chicken) at pretty much any hour—big, fresh, and fast.

BOSTON
Croma
269 Newbury St., 617-247-3200
www.cromaboston.com
pizza style: Neapolitan

New exposed-brick spot with impressive array of thin pizzas—from Margherita to Peking duck—and huge list of wines by the glass.

Ernesto's Pizza
69 Salem St., 617-523-1373
www.ernestosnorthend.com
pizza style: Neapolitan

Ernesto's boasts 31 varieties by the slice or pie.

La Famiglia Giorgio's
112 Salem St., 617-367-6711
www.lafamigliagiorgio.com
pizza style: thick crust

Festive, eternally packed trattoria with *abbondanza* portions, no décor to speak of, and 13 hearty 9-inch pizzas.

Picco
513 Tremont St., 617-927-0066
pizza style: thin crust

Gourmet pizza and ice cream in a retro soda shop. The Alsatian pizza and brownie sundae make perfect late-night, date-night fare.

Pizzeria Regina
11 Thacher St., 617-227-0765
(+12 other locations)
www.pizzeriaregina.com
pizza style: thin crust

Everything about this 1926 landmark is legendary: the red vinyl booths, the long lines, the grumpy waitresses—and the thick-sauced pizzas from a brick oven built in 1888.

Ristorante Fiore
250 Hanover St., 617-371-1176
www.ristorantefiore.com
pizza style: thin crust

A handful of expertly made pizettas, old-style Italian dishes, and wonderful outdoor seating.

T. Anthony
1016 Commonwealth Ave., 617-734-7708
pizza style: New York

Crispy slices of hand-spun pizzas have kept the wooden booths full of BU students since 1976. Recent addition of wireless Internet.

The Upper Crust
20 Charles St., 617-723-9600
(+2 other locations)
www.theuppercrustpizzeria.com
pizza style: Neapolitan

A guy tosses pizza in the front window of this flour-dusted storefront, enticing passersby to check out the slice-of-the-day.

CAMBRIDGE
Cambridge 1
27 Church St., 617-576-1111
pizza style: flatbread

Hipster pizzeria in Harvard Square. The thin, crispy pies are so addictive that (at least) one diehard calls it "crack pizza."

Emma's Pizza
40 Hampshire St., 617-864-8534
pizza style: thin crust

A jovial mix of academics and families toast the creative combos at this local institution, such as dried cranberries with sweet potato.

CHARLESTOWN
Figs
67 Main St., 617-242-2229
(+3 other locations)
pizza style: thin crust

A casual place to sample superstar chef Todd English's oblong pizzas with chi-chi toppings.

EAST BOSTON
Santarpio's
113 Chelsea St., 617-567-9871
pizza style: Boston

This dimly lit bar has become a cult favorite in Eastie for throwback 12-inch white-garlic pizzas.

JAMAICA PLAIN
Bella Luna
403-405 Centre St., 617-524-6060
pizza style: thick crust

Fun pizzeria with a bowling alley and live bands downstairs. The Red Sox-loving owners offer liquefied-cheese pizzas such as the "The Pedro Martinez" with grilled steak and onions.

Pizza Oggi
8 Perkins St., 617-971-9797
(+1 other location)
www.pizzaoggi.com
pizza style: gourmet

Tiny take-out spot run by Steve Welch, whose uncommon passion leads to careful, golden-crusted "Chef Pizzas." In Welch's world, "small" is 16 inches.

NEWTON CENTER
Sweet Tomatoes
47 Langley Rd., 617-558-0222
(+1 other location)
www.sweettomatoespizza.com
pizza style: Neapolitan

Funky, mostly-takeout joint owned by a 20-something named Hedy Jarras. There's no oil in the dough and Jarras uses canned tomatoes.

SPRINGFIELD
Tony's
108 Boston Rd., 413-732-6600
pizza style: medium crust

How can you resist a parlor where the dough is hand-stretched for each order, and the owner believes what makes the pizza special is the customer?

Michigan

ANN ARBOR
Dominick's
812 Monroe, 734-662-5414
pizza style: medium crust
> The best outdoor hangout in Ann Arbor—second-floor balcony, backyard, beer on tap, and fresh sangría. Closed from "the end of UM's football season to after spring break."

New York Pizza Depot
605 E. William St., 734-669-NYPD (6973)
www.newyorkpizzaannarbor.com
pizza style: New York
> NYPD stays open until 4 a.m., and you can kill two cravings with one pie: Order the pasta pizza, featuring the house cheese blend.

Pizza House
618 Church, 734-995-5095
(+1 more location)
www.pizzahouse.com
pizza style: Chicago
> It's a draw between Southwest chicken, vegetarian, and the house special (topped with the usual suspects). Makes 600–1,000 deliveries a day.

DETROIT
Buddy's Pizzeria
17125 Conant St., 313-892-9001
(+8 other locations)
www.buddyspizza.com
pizza style: square deep-dish
> Serving supremely crusty pizzas for 50 years.

PizzaPapalis
553 Monroe St., 313-961-8020
(+8 other locations)
www.pizzapapalis.com
pizza style: Chicago
> Tomatoes from Italy, cheese from Wisconsin, and flour from Kansas come together for boffo deep-dish in an old fur-traders building in Detroit.

FARMINGTON HILLS
Tomatoes Apizza

24369 Halsted Rd., 248-888-4888
(+1 other location)
pizza style: New Haven
> Tomatoes Apizza's maestro, Michael Weinstein, learned his craft on New Haven's Wooster Street and says his crusts are "overcooked" to crispy perfection.

FERNDALE
Como's Restaurant & Pizzeria
22812 Woodward Ave., 248-548-5005
www.comospizza.com
pizza style: Chicago
> Extra festive in warm weather when you can eat outside under striped awnings, Como's best is fresh-tomato with garlic and feta.

LUDINGTON
Chuck Wagon
971 N. Lakeshore Dr., 231-843-2852
pizza style: thickness to order
> Every crust is rolled by hand to the customer's specs at this quaint place where toppings are piled so high, finishing even 1 piece is a challenge.

Sportsman's Restaurant & Irish Pub
111 W. Ludington Ave., 231-843-2138
pizza style: thin crust
> First an Irish pub, then the first pizza place in Ludington. Now a local fave. Secret: They sprinkle paprika on the cheese.

NEW BUFFALO
Brewster's Italian Cafe
11 W. Merchant St., 269-469-3005
pizza style: thin crust
> The owner of charming Brewster's built the wood-burning oven himself and developed his own recipe for semolina herb crust.

STEVENSVILLE
Santaniello's Restaurant
2262 W. Glenlord Rd., 269-429-3966
pizza style: thick crust
> The smell of tomato-basil sauce permeates this cozy parlor, where the crust is thick and crisp and light and airy—all at the same time.

TROY
Alibi
6700 Rochester Rd., 248-879-0014
pizza style: medium crust

Alibi is akin to a North woods cabin where you can cuddle up to your pepperoni in front of a fireplace.

Minnesota

EAGAN
Italian Pie Shoppe
1438 Yankee Doodle Rd., 651-452-4525
(+2 other locations)
www.italianpieshoppe.com
pizza style: Chicago
> Minnesota's quintessential deep-dish pizza joint. Since 1976, the homey wooden booths have been full.

GRAND MARAIS
Sven and Ole's
9 W. Wisconsin St., 218-387-1713
www.svenandoles.com
pizza style: thick crust
> Scandinavian-themed spot with an amazing view of Lake Superior. Full of original pies, such as the popular "Uffda Zah." Try the lutefisk, too.

HIBBING
Sammy's
106 E. Howard St., 218-263-7574
(+23 other locations)
pizza style: New York
> Sammy's has held court in Bob Dylan's hometown since he was in high school. Today it has expanded into other northern states and Canada. Nice buffet on weekdays.

INTERNATIONAL FALLS
Border Bar Pizza Parlor
415 3rd Ave., 218-283-2222
pizza style: thin crust
> Everyone for miles around says the pizza at this old-fashioned dance hall is the best on the border. Live music on weekends.

MINNEAPOLIS
Galactic Pizza
2917 Lyndale Ave S., 612-824-9100
www.galacticpizza.com
pizza style: gourmet
> An eco-friendly newcomer that uses organic ingredients, prints its menu on hemp paper, and delivers in an electric car with the driver dressed like a super hero.

Pizza Lucé
119 N. 4th St., 612-333-7359
(+3 other locations)
www.pizzaluce.com
pizza style: gourmet
> This downtowner is dripping with urban cool, not to mention whole-wheat crusts, vegan options, and well-chosen ingredients from baked potato to Spanish chicken.

Pizza Nea
306 E. Hennepin Ave., 612-331-9298
www.pizzanea.com
pizza style: Neapolitan
> Turns out an honorable thin-crust with dough made at a nearby bagel shop. Sit at the slick pizza bar and watch 'em assemble your pie.

ST. PAUL
Cossetta's Italian Market & Pizzeria
211 Seventh St. W., 651-222-3476
pizza style: New York
> The line is huge at this 94-year-old Twin Cities legend, but so is the crisp hand-tossed pizza.

Davanni's
41 Cleveland Ave. S., 651-690-4848
(+20 other locations)
www.davannis.com
pizza style: Chicago; thin crust
> Well-regarded Twin Cities chain that does killer delivery business with white, deep, thin, and traditional pies.

Punch Neapolitan Pizza
704 Cleveland Ave. S., 651-696-1066
(+2 other locations)
www.punchpizza.com
pizza style: Neapolitan
> Who knew? The Midwest's truest Naples-style pizza is in a strip mall in Minnesota. Every element on the pies at this tiny pizzeria is perfect: velvety mozzarella, acidic San Marzano tomatoes, crisp wood-fired crust.

Red's Savoy Inn and Pizza
421 7th St. E., 651-227-1437
pizza style: thick crust
> With sparkly vinyl banquettes and crooners on the juke, Red's is thick with character. So is the beloved square-cut pizza.

Mississippi

JACKSON
Bravo Italian Restaurant & Bar
4500 I-55 N., 601-982-8111
www.bravobuzz.com
pizza style: thin crust
> An open kitchen sets the tone at this breezy spot with a popular shrimp-and-pesto pizza and a 400-strong wine list.

Miller's Grocery Restaurant
518 E. Capitol St., 601-355-1955
pizza style: medium crust
> Surprise: The place feels like an old grocery store. Bigger surprise. The owner's fave is Philly cheese steak pizza. No surprise: Pepperoni outsells everything 2 to 1.

OXFORD
Old Venice Pizza Company
1112 Van Buren Ave., 662-236-6872
(+2 other locations)
www.oldvenicepizzaco.com
pizza style: medium crust
> A new place in an old building with long list of unusual pies—such as the "Banscueccio" (grilled chicken, cream cheese, jalapeños).

RIDGELAND
Amerigo
6592 Old Canton Rd., 601-977-0563
(+3 other locations)
www.amerigo.net
pizza style: thin crust
> Offbeat pizzas such as "Daddy Crawdaddy" (crawfish tails, red peppers, and cream cheese) and honey in the dough keep this cafe humming.

Soulshine Pizza Factory
5651 Hwy. 25, 601-919-2000
(+1 other location)
www.soulshinepizza.com
pizza style: thin crust
> At this retro hippie spot, customers wear flip-flops and beer is served in Mason jars; there's live music on the weekend, and the Mediterranean pie is always groovy.

Missouri

CHESTERFIELD
Talayna's
68 Four Seasons Shopping Ctr., 314-469-6650
(+4 other locations)
www.talaynas.com
pizza style: St. Louis
> Its name is Yiddish for "Italian," but don't expect gefilte fish pies. It's admirable St. Louis-style pizza in a lovingly decorated strip-mall spot.

CLINTON
Pizza Glen
205 E. Rives Rd., 660-885-8021
pizza style: Chicago
> Legends abound regarding folks who swing hours out of their way to hit this remote pizzeria for a thick-crusted beauty.

COLUMBIA
Shakespeare's Pizza
225 S. 9th St., 573-449-2454
(+1 other location)
www.shakespeares.com
pizza style: thin crust
> Generations of Mizzou students have fond memories of the pizza at this goofy legend. Kids get dough to play with.

INDEPENDENCE
Tim's Pizza
17201 E. US Hwy. 40, 816-478-0777
www.timspizza.com
pizza style: thin crust
> Brothers Tim and Steve Pace run this sports-crazy pizzeria, where they greet customers by name and offer distinctive pies like the "Ballpark," with Polish sausage and sauerkraut.

JEFFERSON CITY
Arris' Pizza Palace
117 W. High St., 573-635-9225
(+1 other location)
pizza style: thin crust
> Across from the Capitol is MO's most addictive Greek pizza with gyro meat, feta, and onions.

KANSAS CITY
D'Bronx Deli
3904 Bell St., 816-531-0550
pizza style: New York

Modeled after the owner's father's NYC deli, D'Bronx is eternally packed with a noisy crowd that swears this is the country's best slice.

Leo's Pizza
408 NW Englewood Rd., 816-453-6666
pizza style: medium crust
25-year-old hole-in-the-wall with consistently gooey provolone and unique red wine-tinged sauce.

Minsky's Pizza
5105 Main St., 816-561-5100
(+10 other locations)
www.minskys.com
pizza style: gourmet
At this proud indie chain, varieties of crust include honey wheat, and toppings run from almonds to zucchini.

Torre's Pizzeria
4112 Pennsylvania Ave., 816-931-3663
(+1 other location)
pizza style: New York
In the heart of happenin' Westport, this rowdy spot offers thick, thin, and medium crust pies—and does all 3 equally well.

Waldo Pizza
7433 Broadway St., 816-363-5242
(+1 other location)
pizza style: Chicago, St. Louis
Employees wear shirts that say "Corporate Pizza Sucks," which is Waldo in a nutshell.

ST. LOUIS
Cusanelli's
705 Lemay Ferry Rd., 314-631-7686
pizza style: St. Louis
An old mom-and-pop fave in a historic house in South St. Louis.

Fortel's Pizza Den
7932 Mackenzie Rd., 314-353-2360
(+8 other locations)
www.fortels.com
pizza style: medium-thin crust
Sisters Shelly and Shannon Fortel—who used to crash in sleeping bags in the storage room as kids—are now VPs at this family-made chain known for sauce-heavy pies.

Imo's Pizza
4479 Forest Park Ave., 314-535-4667
(+ 93 other locations, most in St. Louis area)
www.imospizza.com
pizza style: St. Louis
A tile installer named Ed Imo basically invented St. Louis-style pizza (thin crust, provel, tangy sauce) when he opened Imo's in 1964.

SPRINGFIELD
McSalty's Pizza Cafe
1550 E. Battlefield St., 417-883-4324
pizza style: thin crust
Unique whole-grain crust holds huge amounts of toppings—especially on the supreme "Bear Pie"—at this dim bilevel spot. Funny band on weekend nights.

Montana

BOZEMAN
Colombo's Pizza & Pasta
1003 W. College St., 406-587-5544
pizza style: New York
The owner, Joe Colombo, has no problem with special orders. If you are allergic to flour, he'll whip up a pizza on rice cakes. Or bring in a crust of your choice and he'll use that.

MacKenzie River Pizza Co.
232 E. Main St., 406-587-0055
(+10 other locations)
www.mackenzieriverpizza.com
pizza style: gourmet
Montana's first (and best) upscale pizza place. Amidst rugged, outdoorsy environs, a friendly staff serves challenging pizzas on sourdough or natural-grain crusts.

GREAT FALLS
Howard's Pizza
713 1st Ave. N., 406-453-1212
(+2 other locations)
pizza style: thin crust
A Great Falls tradition for 45 years, Howard's slices its melty, tangy pies into squares. Bonus: Fun Steinhaus bar attached.

HELENA
The Mediterranean Grill
42 S. Park Ave., 406-495-1212
pizza style: thin crust

Newish spot from a Turkish native who makes brick-oven pizzas from scratch, starting with fresh tomatoes delivered by the bushel.

KALISPELL
Moose's Saloon
173 N. Main St., 406-755-2337
www.moosessaloon.com
pizza style: thin crust
At this character-filled saloon, regulars have included governors and Evel Knievel; all drawn to cornmeal-crusted pizza and beers with names like "Moose's Drool."

MISSOULA
The Bridge Bistro
515 S. Higgins Ave., 406-542-0638
(+1 other location)
www.bridgebistro.com
pizza style: thin crust
Couples and families swear by The Bridge's hand-tossed pizzas in this pleasant turn-of-the-century dance hall space.

Zimorino's Red Pies Over Montana
424 N. Higgins Ave., 406-721-7757
(+1 other location)
www.redpiesovermontana.com
pizza style: New York
Two Italian brothers from NYC conquered Missoula with Zim's pizzas' light, fluffy crust. Wait for them in the wine bar.

RED LODGE
Red Lodge Pizza Company
115 S. Broadway Ave., 406-446-3333
www.thepizzaco.com
pizza style: thin crust
Skiers, rodeo fans, and families rub shoulders in this downtown spot. Huge beer selection, funny mailman-inspired pizza names.

WHITE SULPHUR SPRINGS
Stageline Pizza
210 E. Main St., 406-547-3505
(+19 other locations)
pizza style: medium crust
This unique link in a Montana chain shares the building with a movie theatre. If you call ahead, the projectionist will serve you while you watch the movie in a private viewing booth.

Nebraska

FREMONT
Andy's on First
102 North Main St., 402-721-7474
pizza style: thin crust
> Andy Manes gave up on "cutesy" toppings (sauerkraut, pineapple) and went back to the basics (sausage, pepperoni) because that's what people want.

LINCOLN
Isles Pub & Pizza
6232 Havelock Ave., 402-464-1858
pizza style: medium crust
> Loaded with Irish memorabilia from its first incarnation as a pub. The "Leaning Tower of Pizza" (meats and veggies) accounts for 60% of the sales.

Yai Yai's
1423 O St., 402-477-9166
pizza style: thin crust
> Mix and match between 10 cheeses, 6 sauces, and 34 toppings. You'll be sitting in a church pew, so pray it comes out good and slug down one of the 250 microbrews.

OMAHA
Big Fred's Pizza Garden
1101 S. 119th St., 402-333-4414
pizza style: thin crust
> Order a "Goodie Roonie" and you'll get a chicken pizza with a double crust that folds over the top. 8 TV screens should satisfy your sports cravings, too.

Lo Sole Mio
3001 S. 32nd Ave., 402-345-5656
www.losolemio.com
pizza style: medium crust
> Elegant dining room and double-crust pies—especially the one stuffed with potato and hamburger. But after 4 p.m., the pizzas are strictly to go.

Zio's New York Style Pizzeria
7924 W. Dodge Rd., 402-391-1881
(+2 more locations)
pizza style: New York
> There's a plasma TV screen in the floor of the waiting room, so you can watch while you wait to place your order for a chicken pesto pizza.

Nevada

LAS VEGAS
Giovanni's Pizzeria
7380 S. Eastern Ave., 702-896-6050
pizza style: thin crust
> The meatball-and-onion pizza is very popular at this spot, where the owner works side by side with his mother, who won't give him her meatball recipe.

Metro Pizza
1395 E. Tropicana Ave., 702-736-1955
(+2 other locations)
www.metropizza.com
pizza style: any and all
> Irrepressible owners John Arena and Sam Facchini want so badly to conjure up your best memory of your hometown pizza, they will analyze any pizza you bring in and replicate it for you.

Montesano's Italian Restaurant & Deli
3441 W. Sahara Ave., 702-876-0348
(+1 other location)
www.montesanos.com
pizza style: thin crust
> Family pride in family recipes results in pizzas "made from the heart."

New York Pizza & Pasta
2400 S. Jones Blvd., 702-871-1159
pizza style: New York
> New York transplant Jimmy Vesci has an accent that's way thicker than his hand-tossed crust. His slogan: "Real New York pizza for real pizza lovers."

Rocco's New York Italian Deli
1181 S. Buffalo Dr., 702-254-4777
(+1 other location)
pizza style: New York
> A little slice of New York off-the-beaten-tourist-track. Locals come for the Italian cheeses, pastas, and to read the *New York Daily News*.

RENO
Blue Moon Gourmet Pizza
6135 Lakeside Dr., 775-825-1120
pizza style: gourmet
> Reliable smoke-free spot with a small library, a nice patio, and an excellent BBQ chicken pizza.

New Hampshire

HOOKSETT
Mona Lisa's Pizzeria
1560A Hooksett Rd., 603-485-7300
pizza style: Boston
> Boston-style pizza is hand-tossed, like New York, only a little smaller. Not so the flavor. Try not to load too many toppings on its secret blend of cheeses.

KEENE
Papagallos Restaurant
9 Monadnock Hwy., 603-352-9400
www.papagallos.com
pizza style: thin crust
> Colorful Italian-American restaurant known for a brick-oven white pizza sporting ricotta, mozzarella, and feta.

MANCHESTER
Alley Cat Pizzeria
486 Chestnut St., 603-669-4533
pizza style: New York
> Downtown pizza, traditional and offbeat (corn chips as a topping?). Bonus: Take one book and leave one in the library up front.

MERRIMACK
Giorgio's Trattoria
707 Milford Rd., 603-883-7333
pizza style: Hellenic
> Family restaurant with murals imported from Greece. Specialty pan pizzas bulging with Med-tinged toppings, such as marinated steak tips and caramelized onions.

NASHUA
Michael Timothy's Urban Bistro
212 Main St., 603-595-9334
www.michaeltimothys.com
pizza style: thin crust
> Tidy cafe with its own jazz/wine bar and 7 original pizzas: The crust is grilled, then the toppings are added before going under the broiler.

Pizzico Italian Restaurant
7 Harold Dr., 603-897-0696
pizza style: Neapolitan
> The thin-crusted Margherita at this upscale parlor maintains a crunch under its blanket of grated mozzarella, romano, and Gouda.

NEWPORT
Newport Village Pizza
7 S. Main St., 603-863-3400
(+2 other locations)
www.villagepizza.net
pizza style: thin crust
> Family-run pizzeria turning out consistent, straightforward pies since 1975—plus gourmet offerings, including a chicken cordon bleu pizza.

PETERBOROUGH
Acqua Bistro
18 Depot St., 603-924-9905
www.acqua-bistro.com
pizza style: thin crust
> This bistro overlooking the Nuebanusit River has survived a fire and a flood. Its stone-baked pizzas, with toppings such as caramelized onion, grilled chicken, and garlic cream, are considerably less dangerous.

SALEM
Sal's Just Pizza
29 N. Broadway (Rte. 28), 603-894-6767
(+13 other locations)
www.sals-pizza.com
pizza style: Boston
> The 19-inch, 3-lb. cheese pizza is a legend—and it's only $7.99. Sal's produces more than 10,000 pizzas a week for lucky schoolkids.

New Jersey

BRADLEY BEACH
CBO
600 Main, 732-869-9770
pizza style: New York
> This Shore spot has a funky décor, BYO policy, and coal-fired oven to bake the pizzas topped with house-made mozzarella and fresh basil.

FREEHOLD
Federici's Family Italian Restaurant
14 E. Main St., 732-462-1312
www.federicis.com
pizza style: thin crust
> In an industry that brags about hand-tossed crusts, Federici's comes right out and says their pizzas are incredibly thin and crunchy because the crusts are machine rolled.

HOBOKEN
Benny Tudino's
622 Washington St., 201-792-4132
pizza style: thin crust
> The booths are barely big enough for the wagon-wheel-sized pizzas, and slices ($1.75) are so large it takes 2 plates to hold them.

Filippo's Pizzeria
406 Washington St., 201-798-8210
www.filipposofhoboken.com
pizza style: New York
> Owner Lina Centrella is still there every day, and she's 72 years old. Everything is made from scratch and made to order.

OCEAN CITY
Mack & Manco Pizza
12th and Boardwalk, 609-398-0720
(+2 other locations)
www.mackandmancos.com
pizza style: thin crust
> The plain tomato pie has won *Atlantic City Magazine*'s "Best of the Shore" award 20 years running, and the dining room opens up to the ocean.

PRINCETON
Conte's Bar
339 Witherspoon St., 609-921-8041
pizza style: New York
> Profs, students, townies, and little leaguers mix it up in this joint that looks like a finished rec room circa 1950, where the fresh garlic takes up residence in the tomato pies.

RAMSEY
Kinchley's Tavern Incorporated
586 N. Franklin Tpke., 201-934-7777
pizza style: thin crust
> A hole-in-the-wall joint where regular guys belly up to the bar for a sausage, mushroom, and onion combo.

RED BANK
Red Bank Pizza
15 North Bridge Ave., 732-741-9868
www.chiafullo.com
pizza style: thin crust
> The place is tiny and nondescript, and the pizza is nothing fancy either. Just a great combo of chewy crust, tangy sauce, and oozey cheese.

SEASIDE PARK
Maruca's Tomato Pies Inc.
1927 Promenade, 732-793-0707
pizza style: thin crust
> Twin brothers grew up in Trenton, graduated from college, and then returned to the family business, proffering some of the best slices on the Boardwalk.

SECAUCUS
Plaza Pizza
89 Plaza Center, 201-864-0858
pizza style: New York
> George Lioudis runs the front, and his brother Gus cooks up daily specials such as a white pie with spinach, cream sauce, and grilled chicken.

TRENTON
DeLorenzo's Tomato Pies
530 Hudson St., 609-695-9534
pizza style: New York
> No menu. No bathroom. No booze. No credit. Spectacular pizza.

New Mexico

ALBUQUERQUE
Dion's Pizza
10401 Montgomery Blvd. NE., 505-293-7183
(+9 other locations)
www.dionspizza.com
pizza style: New York
> Dion's has a "life-long goal of world-wide pizza domination by the year 3000." So far it's gone from 1 employee to 600-plus and won numerous awards over its 26 years.

Il Vicino
3403 Central N.E., 505-266-7855
(+7 other locations in Colorado, Missouri, Kansas)
www.ilvicino.com
pizza style: thin crust
> The original in this small, slick chain of microbreweries that turns out crisp wood-fired pizzas is in colorful Nob Hill, along old Route 66.

Saggio's
107 Cornell Dr. SE, 505-255-5454
www.saggios.com
pizza style: gourmet
> Years of overdecorating have given this wildly popular college hangout a fun lived-in feel. Order a puffy-crusted Florentine pizza.

LAS CRUCES

Lorenzo's Ristorante Italiano
1750 Calle De Mercado, 505-525-3170
(+2 other locations)
pizza style: gourmet

Sicilian-style family restaurant. Comfy environs, live music, and general bonhomie almost make the pizzas an afterthought. They shouldn't be.

SANTA FE

Upper Crust Pizza
329 Old Santa Fe Trail, 505-982-0000
www.uppercrustpizza.com
pizza style: gourmet

This old adobe house is legendary in Santa Fe for whole-wheat crust pizza. 2 former grade-school buddies serve creative pies and host live music nightly.

TAOS

Taos Pizza Out Back
712 N. Pueblo Rd., 505-758-3112
pizza style: gourmet

Organic, wood-burning pizza. The ski town vibe is laid-back—crayons and paper for the kids—but high prices have caused locals to dub it "The Setback."

New York

BRONX

Nick's Pizza
1356 E. Gun Hill Rd., 718-652-6500
pizza style: New York

The quintessential neighborhood joint: a few tables in a plain storefront but a slice of tomato pie that puts a spring in your step.

Tosca Café
4038 E. Tremont Ave., 718-239-3300
www.toscanyc.com
pizza style: New York

Owner of a 1922 coal-fired oven, this former bakery is now an Italian-American restaurant serving thin, blistery pizzas.

BROOKLYN

DiFara Pizza
1424 Avenue J, 718-258-1367
pizza style: Neapolitan

Good things are worth waiting for—and the pizzas at DiFara's are very good, indeed. Dominic

De Marco painstakingly makes every perfectly balanced, chewy/crispy pie himself, using a coal oven, a 3-mozzarella blend, and a drizzle of oil.

Grimaldi's
19 Old Fulton St., 718-858-4300
(+1 New Jersey location)
www.grimaldis.com
pizza style: New York

This legendary parlor under the Brooklyn Bridge used to deliver pizza to Ole Blue Eyes in Hoboken. Now Sinatra croons on tape while customers moon over tomato-basil pie.

L & B Spumoni Gardens
2725 86th St., 718-372-8400
www.spumonigardens.com
pizza style: Sicilian

In 1939 Ludivico Barbati opened a spumoni store (2¢ a scoop) to help out one of his sons. In short order he added his other 2 sons to the payroll and Sicilian pizza—made with the cheese on top of the sauce—to the menu.

Lenny's Pizza of Brooklyn Incorporated
1969 86th St., 718-946-1292
pizza style: New York

The signature pie topped with basil, grated cheese, olive oil, and marinara sauce is called "Grandma Pizza."

Totonno Pizzeria Napolitano
1524 Neptune Ave., 718-372-8606
(+3 other locations)
www.totonnos.com
pizza style: New York

This Coney Island legend opened in 1924 and remodeled in 1952, when the color turquoise must have been all the rage. But the pizzas are still a kick—thin, crisp crusts with mozzarella oozing all over the place.

BUFFALO

Bocce Club Pizza
4174 N. Bailey Ave., 716-833-1344
(+1 other location)
www.bocceclubpizza.com
pizza style: medium crust

Here, 18 ovens make 36 pizzas at a time and produce thousands for carryout every weekend. Everyone talks about the hand-cut pepperoni.

CONGERS

Nicky's II
48 Lake Rd., 845-268-5800
pizza style: medium crust

This strip-mall parlor hand tosses its ever-popular "plain cheese"; the memorable difference must be the secret blend of spices that goes into the sauce.

ITHACA

The Nines
311 College Ave., 607-272-1888
pizza style: Chicago

According to owner Mark Kielmann, "Raised-crust deep-dish pizza is our claim to fame. Each one is cut into 4 great big squares." Toppings? "Gourmet, shmourmet," he says. "Pepperoni is most popular."

NEW YORK CITY

Angelo's Pizzeria
117 W. 57th St., 212-333-4333
pizza style: New York

The coal-oven pizzas get Peter Reinhart's significant stamp of approval in *American Pie*.

APizz
217 Eldridge St., 212-253-9199
www.apizz.com
pizza style: Neapolitan

Crowded trattoria dominated by hipsters and a giant wood-fired oven. Its thin rectangular pies are burning up the Lower East Side.

Arturo's Pizza
1610 York Ave., 212-288-2430
pizza style: New York

Cramped joint with a handful of red-and-white checked tables on the Upper East Side. The coal-oven pizza has been exactly the same since 1957.

Bella Blu
967 Lexington Ave., 212-988-4624
www.bellabluny
pizza style: gourmet

Boisterous Italian spot known for more than pizza, but the blue ceramic wood-burning oven turns out terrific thin-crust pies.

Famous Ray's Pizza
465 6th Ave., 212-243-2253
pizza style: New York

There are dozens of pretenders to Ray's Manhattan throne, but this is the true original. The slices are huge and floppy: ideal for the New York "fold-hold."

Giorgione
307 Spring St., 212-352-2269
pizza style: **Neapolitan**
Giorgio DeLuca, of Dean & DeLuca fame, pulls the strings at this noisy TriBeCa haunt with a wood-burning stove.

Gonzo
140 W. 13th St., 212-645-4606
pizza style: **thin crust**
In this noisier-than-hell West Village trattoria, the high ceilings—painted Renaissance-style—are almost as striking as the grilled pizzas.

Joe's Pizza
233 Bleecker St., 212-366-1182
pizza style: **New York**
Quintessential by-the-slice spot in the Village. The original location down the street has closed, but the tangy sauce and yeasty thin crust can still be had here.

John's Pizzeria
278 Bleecker St., 212-243-1680
www.johnsofbleeckerstreet.com
pizza style: **New York**
The 100-year-old brick oven is older than the place itself, but the pizzas still inspire carved-out memories in the time-worn wooden booths of this NYC legend.

Lombardi's
32 Spring St., 212-941-7994
www.lombardispizza.com
pizza style: **New York**
When America's granddaddy of pizza parlors stoked its first coal-oven pizza in 1905, little did Gennaro Lombardi know that he was changing the culinary landscape of his adopted country forever.

Mariella Pizza
960 8th Ave., 212-757-3016
pizza style: **New York**
According to owner John Licata, what you need for good pizza is a spicy sauce made from great tomatoes.

Otto Enoteca and Pizzeria
1 5th Ave., 212-995-9559

www.ottopizzeria.com
pizza style: **gourmet**
In this sunny room, superchef Mario Batali serves a light, pale thin-crust pie cooked on a flat iron griddle with ingredients such as shaved fennel and bottarga. Not for purists—but everyone else loves them.

Patsy's
2287 1st Ave., 212-534-9783
(+7 other locations)
pizza style: **New York**
New Yorkers are devoted to the textbook coal-oven slices at this historic hole in East Harlem.

Pizza 33
201 E. 33rd St., 212-545-9191
(+2 other locations)
pizza style: **thin crust**
There's a giant cupid hanging from the ceiling at this obsessively clean late-night spot, but the real bull's-eye is the pizza Margherita.

Two Boots
44 Ave. A, 212-254-1919
(+6 other locations)
www.twoboots.com
pizza style: **Cajun**
The "boots" are Italy and Louisiana, which gives you some idea of what to expect: cornmeal crust, peppery sauce, and swampland toppings such as BBQ shrimp, crawfish, and andouille.

Una Pizza Napoletana
349 E. 12th St., 212-477-9950
pizza style: **Neapolitan**

TOP 10

Owner Anthony Mangieri's brick-oven pizzas (made with rare Sicilian sea salt) are as authentic as it gets. His East Village temple is open Thursday–Sunday until he runs out of fresh dough.

NANUET
Martios
171 Main St., 845-623-9574
pizza style: **thin crust**
This cozy spot has stained-glass lamps hanging over the wooden benches and tables. The wood-fired oven is reserved for the individual pizzas.

PORT WASHINGTON
Salvatore's
124 Shore Rd., 516-883-8457
pizza style: **New York**
Fred Lacagnina, a nephew of Patsy Lancieri (of Patsy's fame), runs his pizzeria the old-school

way: with a coal-fired brick oven, proffering no slices, accepting no credit cards.

QUEENS
Nick's Pizza
108-26 Ascan Ave., 718-263-1126
(+1 other location)
pizza style: **thin crust**
Everyone waxes fanatic about the crust at this spacious neighborhood joint: Blistered along one edge, it stays miraculously crisp.

ROSLYN
Joanne's Gourmet Pizza & Pasta
1067 Northern Blvd., 516-869-8686
(+1 other location)
www.joannesgourmetpizza.com
pizza style: **Sicilian**
Proprietor Rino DiMaria pulled a driver from a burning car outside Joanne's in 2003, an act only slightly more heroic than the 36 varieties of pizza he's been pulling from the oven since he was a kid.

STATEN ISLAND
Goodfella's
1718 Hylan Blvd., 718-987-2422
(+ 10 other locations)
www.goodfellas.com
pizza style: **thin crust**
A cop, a carpet cleaner, and a cosmetics salesman teamed up in 1993 to open this pizzeria. A zillion awards later, the brick-oven "Pizza alla Vodka" is still the best reason to visit Staten Island.

TROY
I Love NY Pizza
125 Fourth St., 518-274-0071
www.ilovenypizza.com
pizza style: **New York**
This late-night dive with the gruff staff is a legend for instant gratification in the capital area.

VALLEY COTTAGE
The Pie Man
107 N. Route 303, Brookside Ave.
845-268-8797
pizza style: **thin crust**
Everyone falls in love with the Have-It-Your-Way pizza.

VOORHEESVILLE
Smith's Tavern
112 Maple Ave., 518-765-4163

pizza style: thin crust

"Smitty's" is a small-town family tavern with top-notch white pizzas, a kid-friendly atmosphere, and a disturbingly large collection of gnomes.

WANTAGH
Cherrywood Pizza Inc.
1919 Wantagh Ave., 516-826-3077
pizza style: New York

"Pat's Special" isn't on the menu, but if the owner, Pat Tuzzolo, is around, he'll make one for you: garlic, tomato, mozzarella, oregano.

Spassos Pizzeria
1159 Wantagh Ave., 516-785-8560
pizza style: thin crust

This rustic parlor has 80 years of pizza knowledge—starting in Sicily—behind it. Student special: 2 slices and a soda for $3.25.

WATERVLIET
The Purple Pub
2 Cohoes Rd., 518-273-9646
pizza style: "kind of like Sicilian"

It doesn't look like much, but this cheapo Italian-American hangout has been cranking out some of the area's best pizzas for more than 30 years.

North Carolina

ASHEVILLE
Marco's Pizzeria
946 Merrimon Ave., 828-285-0709
(+1 other location)
pizza style: New York

Marco Lacagnina is a cousin of New York's famed Patsy Lancieri, and, hence, of royal pizza lineage; his stone-oven offering has a perfect thin crust.

CHAPEL HILL
Pepper's Pizza
127 E. Franklin St., 919-967-7766
pizza style: gourmet

Students go wild for Pepper's, though it's more ambitious than the usual college-town pizzeria. Local artwork, colorful staff, and great white pizza.

CHARLOTTE
Brixx Pizza
1801 Scott Ave., 704-376-1000
(+5 other locations)

www.brixxpizza.com
pizza style: thin crust

Yuppie pizza in a laid-back, tree-lined neighborhood. Sit on the patio to chow on wood-fired pizzas (spinach and artichoke dip, for example) and sample the wonderful beer list.

Fuel Pizza Cafe
1501 Central Ave., 704-376-3835
(+5 other locations)
www.fuelpizza.com
pizza style: New York

Original pizzeria in a former gas station. Décor includes filling-station tchotchkes, and the pizzas, with names such as "The Whole Engine," lean to New York-style.

Wolfman Pizza
106 S. Sharon Amity Rd., 704-377-4695
(+4 other locations)
pizza style: California

This local hit serves offbeat ingredients such as Gruyère, oysters, and peanuts—and a pizza called "The Led Zeppelin."

GREENSBORO
Elizabeth's Pizza
2116 Lawndale Dr., 336-370-0800
(+7 other locations)
www.elizabethpizza.com
pizza style: Neapolitan, Sicilian

Founded by the Naples-born Errichiello family. Always packed, always open, always consistent.

New York Pizza
337 Tate St., 336-272-8953
pizza style: New York

UNCG students cried when New York Pizza caught on fire in 2002. But it came back strong with its good honest pie and live bands.

Pieworks
3700 Lawndale Dr., 336-282-9003
(+5 other locations)
www.pieworks.com
pizza style: gourmet

More than 80 smart, inventive pizzas line the menu here, which includes 150 toppings from rattlesnake to snow peas. Keg root beer sweetens the deal.

RALEIGH
Brothers Pizza
2508 1/2 Hillsborough St., 919-832-3664
pizza style: thin crust

Another college-town anchor, cooking on stone for almost 40 years in the shadow of N.C. State.

Lilly's Pizza
1813 Glenwood Ave., 919-833-0226
www.lillyspizza.com
pizza style: gourmet

This hipster joint named for an owner's dog has won countless awards, all with a crust made of organic wheat flour. Good music, nice patio, and a sense of humor—on the toppings menu, listed under "fruits and nuts": "The Staff."

WEAVERVILLE
Underwood Baking Company
369 Ox Creek Rd., 828-768-1002
pizza style: thin crust

Michael Olivier built his own European-style brick oven for this farm bakery. Every Friday night (seasonally), he bakes giant organic sourdough pizzas for $10 each with toppings that were grown on the farm.

WILMINGTON
Numero Uno Pizza
204 Princess St., 910-763-1156
pizza style: New York

Hole-in-the-wall along the Cape Fear coast that does commendable NY-style pizza and stromboli.

WINSTON-SALEM
Mario's Pizza
1066 Hanes Mall Blvd., 336-768-0057
(+3 other locations)
www.mariospizza.org
pizza style: New York

The 22-inch slices are so big you can't get 'em takeout because Mario's doesn't have a box big enough.

North Dakota

BISMARCK
A & B Pizza
311 S. 7th St., 701-222-3108
(+2 other locations)
pizza style: thin crust

Home-grown pizzeria with fresh-made pies—such as the taco pizza—cut into squares.

FARGO

Gina's Pizza
2630 S. University Dr., 701-297-8000
(+1 other location)
pizza style: Chicago, New York
Proffers distinctive thin crust, New York-style, or deep-dish out of South Fargo's most famous bowling alley. Try the bacon-cheeseburger pizza.

Santa Lucia
505 40th St. SW, 701-281-8656
pizza style: medium crust
Off-the-beaten-track, this tavern-style parlor boasts Greek pizzas. Spanako (spinach, feta, and onions combined with dill and olive oil) sets the standard.

GRAND FORKS

Popolino's Pizza
1505 11th Ave N., 701-746-7677
pizza style: New York
Known for the XXXL-sized "Jumbolino" pizza and offbeat varieties such as "Hot Wing" pizza with hot sauce and chicken. Delivery only.

Ohio

BEXLEY

Bexley Pizza Plus
2540 E. Main St., 614-237-3305
www.bexleypizzaplus.com
pizza style: medium crust
Bexley's "Ultimate" pizza, with 2 different kinds of pepperoni and 2 different kinds of mushrooms, won the 2003 Mid America Pizza Pizzazz contest. Strictly pickup and delivery.

CINCINNATI

Dewey's Pizza
3014 Madison Rd., 513-731-7755
(+5 other locations)
www.deweyspizza.com
pizza style: New York
A pizza parlor with heart: A view of pizza chefs tossing the dough; 8 beers on tap; grown-up pies with whimsical names.

Pizza Tower
8945 Governors Way, 513-683-8400
www.pizzatower.com
pizza style: regular, between thick and thin
There are 4 stories in the contemporary Italian-styled tower, with one floor featuring a cartoons-only TV screen dedicated to kids.

Pomodori's Pizzeria
121 W. McMillan St., 513-861-0080
(+1 other location)
www.pomodoris.com
pizza style: thin
The old building is steps from UC, and it's famous for a wood-fired, veggie-laden pie anchored by sautéed artichoke hearts and topped with capers and pesto.

CLEVELAND

Antonio's Pizza & Spaghetti
7401 W. Ridgewood Dr., 440-886-2511
(+4 express stores)
pizza style: Chicago
They make thin crusts, too, but deep-dish is the *raison d'être*. The pepperoni deluxe has been described as a life-transforming experience.

Geraci's Restaurant
2266 Warrensville Ctr. Rd., 216-371-5643
pizza style: Sicilian
The crust is made from raised dough but the pie is round and cut into slices. So good it's won *Cleveland* magazine's Silver Spoon award 8 times.

Mama Santa's Restaurant and Pizzeria
12305 Mayfield Rd., 216-231-9567
pizza style: medium crust
Grandma Santa founded the place in 1961. Today her grandson makes the dough, his wife makes the sauce, and the recipes remain family secrets.

COLUMBUS

Adriatico's New York Style
265 W. 11th Ave., 614-421-2300
(+1 other location)
pizza style: Chicago
Cases of beer, pop, and tomato paste are stacked right next to the benches in this beloved college joint. The 18-by-24-inch "Inflation Fighter" weighs almost 15 lbs.

Michael's Pizza & Pasta
3331 Maize Rd. 614-261-9091
pizza style: thin crust
The owner's daughters are named Sierra and Sulaca—and so are his 2 favorite pizzas. We won't tell you who created the cinnamon-sprinkled one topped with pineapple, almonds, coconut.

Rotolo's Pizza
1749 W. 5th Ave., 614-488-7934
(+3 other locations)
www.rotolospizza.com
pizza style: medium crust
The friendliest carryout in Columbus sells a ton of homemade meatball-and-banana-pepper pizzas.

Courtesy of Marion's Piazza

DAYTON

Marion's Piazza
3443 N. Dixie Dr., 937-277-6553
(+6 other locations)
pizza style: thin crust
Thanks to the skylight and al fresco décor, you can pretend you are in an Italian courtyard while you gobble the "Deluxe" pizza. Bonus: 300 celeb photos cover the walls.

TOLEDO

Original Gino's Pizza & Spaghetti
3981 Monroe St., 419-472-3567
(+3 other locations)
www.originalginos.com
pizza style: medium crust
Generations of UT students have gone wild for Gino's specialty pizzas: Cajun, Hawaiian, chili, Reuben, taco.

WARREN

Sunrise Inn
506-510 E. Market St., 330-392-5176
www.thesunriseinn.com
pizza style: pan
A straight-up spot where the buttery (but ungreasy) pies are topped with a generous sprinkling of Parmesan and Romano.

Courtesy of Pizzicato Gourmet Pizza and Tracy Frankel; Courtesy of Old Town Pizza

Oklahoma

ANTLERS
High Street Pizza
226 N. High St., 580-298-5511
pizza style: gourmet

Unique spot in a friendly small town where the regulars take home loaves of bread and the tabletops are cut from old bowling lanes. Best seller: taco pizza.

NORMAN
JJ's Pizza Stop
530 W. Lindsey St., 405-360-0500
pizza style: medium crust

Family pictures line the walls of this spot on the edge of OU. Owner Jim Brooks knows his pizzas are good because he's "never had 1 complaint."

OKLAHOMA CITY
Hemi's Pizza and Grill
3500 N. Classen Blvd., 405-528-6444
www.hemispizza.com
pizza style: stuffed

The name means "Here Every Meal Is Special," and the pizzas prove it: expert offerings made with fresh dough, and a 28-inch beast that requires 24 hours' notice.

STILLWATER
Hideaway Pizza
230 S. Knoblock St., 405-372-4777
(+7 other locations)
www.hideawaypizza.com
pizza style: thin crust

One look at the shadowbox ceiling and collection of kites, and you know this place—Oklahoma's oldest pizzeria—is a college legend. On game days, the line snakes down the block.

WALTERS
Patman's Pizza
214 S. Broadway St., 580-875-3979
pizza style: Chicago

Rhonda Hatfield's converted fast food drive-in is across the street from the local school; at lunchtime every kid in town rushes over for a slice of pepperoni.

Oregon

EUGENE
Ambrosia
174 E. Broadway, 541-342-4141
pizza style: thin crust

The mesquite in the wood-fired oven brings out flavors like fennel-flecked sausage and olive oil-marinated artichoke hearts.

Pizza Research Institute
1328 Lawrence St., 541-343-1307
pizza style: medium crust

The owners of this funky-chic vegetarian pie house call their product "Northwest artisan." Their vege-head devotees dig the house-made, tofu-based, ricotta-style cheese.

HAWTHORNE
Hot Lips Pizza
1909 SW 6th Ave., 503-224-0311
(+3 more locations)
www.hotlipspizza.com
pizza style: New York

This politically correct, hallowed college spot (Portland State U) uses fresh, locally grown ingredients—house-pickled organic jalapeños, free-range chicken.

PORTLAND
Escape From New York Pizza
622 NW 23rd Ave., 503-227-5423
pizza style: thin crust

One regular describes the city's first by-the-slice spot as "Portland cluttered kitsch." No matter. When it comes to pizza, it's dedicated to the basics: pepperoni and cheese.

Flying Pie Pizzeria
7804 SE Stark St., 503-254-2016
(+3 other locations)
www.flying-pie.com
pizza style: "everything but Chicago"

Owner Ty Dupuis, 3-time winner of the fastest dough-maker title at the International Pizza Expo, can spin 5 "skins" faster than you can eat 1 of his 11-lb., 18-inch combo supremes.

The Mississippi
3552 N. Mississippi St., 503-288-3231
www.mississippipizza.com
pizza style: New York

Who could resist a "Greek Geek" pizza in a room that features a Klezmer band on a street named Mississippi in Oregon?

Oasis Cafe
3701 SE Hawthorne Blvd., 503-231-0901
pizza style: medium crust

Oasis sells lots of veggie and vegan pies, and every one is drizzled with garlic butter fresh out of the brick-lined oven.

Old Town Pizza
226 NW Davis, 503-222-9999
www.oldtownpizza.com
pizza style: medium crust

The Shanghai Tunnels that run under the century-old building reek of lore—something about kidnapped sailors in the 1800s. Their ghosts supposedly haunt the pizzeria, which makes for great conversation over a fresher-than-fresh pesto pizza.

Pizzicato Gourmet Pizza
505 NW 23rd Ave., 503-242-0023
(+15 other locations)
www.pizzicatogourmetpizza.com
pizza style: gourmet

This sophisticated parlor offers puttanesca for vege-heads, quattro formaggi for the un-restrained, and squisita (lamb sausage, 3 cheeses, pesto, and more) for the cheeky chic.

Pennsylvania

ARDMORE

Peace A Pizza
4 Station Rd., 610-896-4488
(+6 other locations)
www.peacepizza.com
pizza style: thick crust
At this kid-friendly chain, cheese and spices are baked right in to the thick crust of the 20-inch pies. Toppings include bacon cheeseburger and baked ziti.

HAZLETON

Alta Pizzeria & Pasta House
380 S. Poplar St., 570-455-7892
pizza style: square, thin crust
Aniello Chirico's sauce recipe comes from a village south of Salerno, the square crust is his grandmother's tradition, and his 2 favorite pies, "Francesca" and "Maria Rosa," are named for his daughters.

OLD FORGE

Revello's Pizza
502 S. Main St., 570-457-9843
www.revellos.com
pizza style: Old Forge
In Old Forge, you order a tray, not a pie, and the rectangular pieces are called cuts, not slices.

Salerno's
139 Moosic Road, 570-457-9920
pizza style: Old Forge
This Italian-feeling spot upholds the Old Forge tradition of rectangular cuts, topped with a "really creamy" blend of American and a mystery Italian cheese.

PHILADELPHIA

Gianfranco Pizza Rustica
6 N. Third St., 215-592-0048
pizza style: New York
Pictures of old Philadelphia line the stucco walls of this tiny place that goes through 200 lbs. of chicken a week making "Chicken-Ranch" pizza.

Lorenzo & Son Pizza
305 South St., 215-627-4110
pizza style: New York
Don't bother waiting for a table here; just fold up your giant blackened crispy-crust slice (cheese or pepperoni only) and take in the neighborhood scene.

Mama Palma's
2229 Spruce St., 215-735-7357
pizza style: Neapolitan
Gaze at the fireplace or watch the pizza being made right in front of you. Bite into a pizza Margherita and you're going to think you are in Naples.

Marra's Restaurant
1734 E. Passyunk Ave., 215-463-9249
pizza style: Neapolitan
Bianca, pescatore, ortolana: Any pizza made in the 78-year-old oil-fueled oven has got to be good—the bricks are made from the volcanic ash-rich clay around Mt. Vesuvius.

Pietro's
121-123 South St., 215-733-0675
(+2 other locations)
www.pietrospizza.com
pizza style: New York
Pietro's owner, Peter Pahialis, believes that a superhot coal oven does the trick for amazingly crispy pizza.

Tacconelli's
2604 E. Somerset St., 215-425-4983
pizza style: thin crust
Tacconelli's pizza rivals the best of New Haven and New York—and there's only one way to get one. Call a day ahead to reserve your dough.

PITTSBURGH

Mineo's Pizza House
2128 Murray Ave., 412-521-9864
(+1 other location)
www.mineospizza.com
pizza style: medium crust
The Mineo brothers make the pizza exactly the way their dad did when he opened in 1958: tangy sweet sauce, plenty of cheese, and oodles of toppings. Little Caesars and Domino's both came to Murray Avenue, but didn't stay long.

Photograph: Christopher Lowry

Vincent's Pizza Park
998 Ardmore Blvd., 412-271-9181
pizza style: thick
"Vinnie" pies are legendary for their rich crusts. The owner, Vinnie Chianese, is full of tough-guy mottos and moxie—but, like his crusty pizzas, he's a softy underneath.

STATE COLLEGE

Hi-Way Pizza
1688 N. Atherton St., 814-237-0375
(+2 other locations)
www.dantesinc.com
pizza style: Neapolitan
Sponge-painted walls and landscape murals provide the backdrop for exceptionally flaky-crusted pizza made from croissant dough.

Rhode Island

NARRAGANSETT

Pier Pizza
13 Pier Market Pl., 401-792-9393
(+3 other locations)
www.pierpizza.com
pizza style: New York
Vacation fave across from a beach serving giant gourmet slices for surfers and URI students.

PROVIDENCE

Al Forno
577 S. Main St., 401-273-9760
www.alforno.com
pizza style: thin crust
The "inventor" of grilled pizza in the early eighties, Al Forno boasts nationally applauded chefs who have attracted a slew of awards and curious diners to this ivy-sheltered spot.

Bob and Timmy's Grilled Pizza
32 Spruce St., 401-453-2221
pizza style: thin crust
> Mega-thin gourmet pizzas are the currency at this casual spot that rides Al Forno's grilled pizza wave. Patio with views of a park.

Caserta Pizzeria
121 Spruce St., 401-272-3618
pizza style: Neapolitan
> John Campagnone's basic, rectangular pies have been a legend in this old Italian neighborhood since 1946.

Fellini Pizzeria
166 Wickenden St., 401-751-6737
pizza style: thin crust
> The tables are hogged by college kids—all eating the crisp, whole wheat-crusted pies—day and night at this funky spot.

Sicilia's
181 Atwells Ave., 401-273-9222
pizza style: Chicago
> Sicilia's illustrious stuffed pizzas take an hour to make. But a 2-inch-tall gooey/crusty behemoth is an end that justifies the means.

South Carolina

CHARLESTON
Andolini's Pizza
82 Wentworth St., 843-722-7437
(+2 other locations)
www.andolinis.com
pizza style: New York
> The eclectic crowd at this downtown spot is unfazed by the wacky depictions of Elvis Presley and Jesus Christ, but gets into hand-tossed faves topped with garlic and meatballs.

Blossom
171 E. Bay St., 843-722-9200
www.magnolias-blossom-cypress.com/blossom
pizza style: gourmet
> There are only a few pizzas on the menu, but the likes of the wood-roasted citrus-marinated shrimp pie proves less is more.

Gilroy's Pizza Pub
353 King St., 843-937-9200
pizza style: medium crust
> It's taken this downtown joint less than a

decade to look like it's been around forever. The college crowd thrives on bacon-double-cheeseburger pizza until 4 a.m.

Sharky's Pizza
306 King St., 843-722-7200
pizza style: New York
> The new owners gussied up the joint before rolling out their great-grandfather's 100-year-old recipe. Crispy crusts, doughy rims: pure New York.

GREENVILLE
Bertolo's Pizza
200 N. Main St., 864-467-9555
(+1 other location)
pizza style: New York
> This spiffy downtown parlor grooves on its made-from-scratch pies, and the residential renaissance has turned the place into a neighborhood haunt.

Frodo's Pizza
511 S. Pleasantburg Dr., 864-232-1800
(+3 other locations)
www.frodospizza.com
pizza style: Chicago
> You gotta like a place named for a Hobbit. Happy fans go back for the terrific sauce, serious toppings, and eccentric atmosphere.

Gourmet Pizza & More
2016 Augusta St., 864-232-6222
pizza style: thick crust
> This neighborhood hang has a strong following for its thick—but crisp—crust and generous toppings.

South Dakota

MADISON
Skipper's
204 S. Egan Ave., 605-256-4986
pizza style: thin crust
> A deceased founder named Cletus... an old sloping floor... square-cut pizzas named after locals with tags like "Gooner"... a professionally trained chef/owner who lives upstairs: Skipper's is a true American original.

SIOUX FALLS
Minerva's
301 S. Phillips Ave., 605-334-0386
(+7 other locations)

http://minervas.net
pizza style: gourmet
> Popular all-American chain that serves zany pizzas, such as a roasted potato pie with ranch dressing, scallions, bacon, and 3 kinds of cheese.

YANKTON
Charlie's Pizza House
804 Summit St., 605-665-2212
pizza style: medium crust
> The oldest pizzeria in South Dakota. "It's probably the best I've had anywhere in the U.S.," says Bernie Hunhoff, editor of *South Dakota* magazine.

Tennessee

ANTIOCH
Picnic Pizza
2713 Murfreesboro Rd., 615-399-0010
www.picnicpizza.net
pizza style: New York
> The spicy pizza at this 36-seater sounds insanely hot: jalapeños, banana peppers, crushed red pepper. Guess the garlic is there to take the edge off.

FRANKLIN
Guido's New York Pizzas
600A Frazier Dr., 615-503-9626
www.guidosnypizzas.com
pizza style: thin crust
> Guido's has earned the respect of NY pizza gourmands on 3 counts: It's in a really cool converted warehouse, there's live jazz on weekends, the crust is like back home.

Pie in the Sky Pizza
1770 Galleria Blvd., 615-778-0988
www.pieintheskypizza.com
pizza style: thick crust
> The rocket ship motif isn't overdone, thankfully. Most everyone launches their taste buds with the spiral breadsticks made of pizza dough, cheese, and garlic.

HERMITAGE
Vinny's Pizza
4414 Lebanon Pike, 615-874-2224
(+1 other location)
www.vinnyspizza.biz
pizza style: Chicago
> For discounts and freebies, come Wednesday

in costume, Thursday in pajamas, Saturdays—oh heck, check the Web site.

MEMPHIS

Coletta's Italian Restaurant
1063 S. Parkway E., 901-948-7652
(+1 other location)
www.colettasrestaurant.com
pizza style: medium crust

Claims to fame: It's the oldest restaurant in Memphis; BBQ pizza originated here; Elvis had the good sense to love the mountain of tender pork held together by rich tangy 'que sauce.

Memphis Pizza Cafe
2087 Madison Ave., 901-726-5343
(+3 other locations)
www.memphispizzacafe.com
pizza style: thin crust

Voted the best pizza for 10 years in a row by *The Memphis Flyer*. Known for super-thin crust—particularly the one topped with blackened chicken.

NASHVILLE

Christopher Pizza Co.
1524-A Demonbreun St., 615-742-7464
www.christopherpizza.com
pizza style: medium crust

This indie, with its great sense of humor and taste, has a menu full of silly-sounding pies—such as "The Little White Lie"—and a hip clientele happy to munch on "Humdingers" and listen to live music into the wee hours.

DaVinci's Gourmet Pizza
1812 Hayes St., 615-329-8098
www.davincisgourmetpizza.com
pizza style: gourmet

Picture yourself sipping Chianti in the courtyard of a 1920s Southern cottage. Add an Etta James soundtrack and a smoked oyster pizza.

House of Pizza
15 Arcade, 615-242-7144
(+1 other location)
pizza style: New York

The owners, transplanted New Yawkers, dish out abuse with the pizza at this downtown institution, but no one seems to mind.

Mafiaoza's Pizzeria
2400 12th Ave. S., 615-269-4646
www.mafiaozas.com

pizza style: New York

Crunchy thin pizza with wild toppings (scallops, eggplant), especially on Tuesday nights when 2 slices go for the price of 1; ditto for the beer. The patio is rigged so you can eat outside even on chilly nights.

Texas

AUSTIN

Frank & Angie's Pizzeria
508 West Ave., 512-472-3534
pizza style: New York

Singular pies piled with everything from crisp baby spinach leaves to Italian meatballs.

Mangia Chicago Stuffed Pizza
3500 Guadalupe St., 512-302-5200
(+2 other locations)
pizza style: stuffed

Stuffed pizza, made with typical Midwestern toppings or paved with veggies only; either way, the tomato sauce is all hopped up with garlic.

Reale's Pizza & Cafe
13450 N. Hwy. 183, 512-335-5115
www.realespizzaandcafe.com
pizza style: thin crust

Frank and Dino are on the soundtrack at this trattoria where Chianti bottles line the walls and perfect strangers trade slices.

CARROLLTON

Joe's Pizza Pasta & Subs
1904 E. Belt Line Rd., 972-416-6555
pizza style: New York

A tribute to NYC and its pizza: counter service, wooden tables, and a painting of the World Trade Center.

DALLAS

Arcodoro
2708 Routh St. 214-871-1924
(+1 other location)
www.arcodoro.com
pizza style: gourmet

The Farris brothers pay homage to their Sardinian roots with designer pizzas—and endless other regional delicacies—in this stunning spot in the Uptown district.

Campisi's Egyptian Lounge
5610 E. Mockingbird Ln., 214-827-0355
(+5 other locations)
http://campisis.us
pizza style: thin crust

If you're into *The Sopranos*, try to snag a table in the original Mafia-modish dining room. The rectangular pizzas have plenty of personality, too.

Fireside Pies
2820 N. Henderson Ave., 214-370-3916
pizza style: gourmet

Smart new boutique pizzeria where the open kitchen churns out hefty wood-fired pies with thick-sliced tomatoes and organic toppings.

DENTON

The Tomato Pizza in a Pan
1226 W. Hickory, 940-383-1111
pizza style: thick crust

The place borders on grungy, but all types gather on the upstairs deck after the bars have closed. A hefty slice, with its 2 layers of cheese, has a bonding effect on the crowd.

HOUSTON

Cafe Botticelli
306 Gray St., 713-533-1140
pizza style: New York

Best of 2 worlds: hipster wine bar (espresso and fortified coffees galore) and authentic NY-style pizza (try the olive oil/garlic-glazed pies).

LEANDER

Saccone's Pizza
2701-A South Hwy. 183, 512-259-1882
(+1 other location)
www.saccones.com
pizza style: New York

Deep in the heart of Texas, a trio of Northeasterners run a mom-and-pop Jersey pizza shop.

LONGVIEW

Pizza King
1100 E. Marshall Ave., 903-753-0912
www.pizza-king.9601185328004.
worldpages-ads.com
pizza style: thin crust

Done up like a 1950s diner, this parlor slow-cooks its pizza, but the crowd agrees it's worth the wait.

SAN ANTONIO
Main Street Pizza & Pasta
1906 N. Main Ave., 210-732-8861
(+1 other location)
www.mainstreetsa.com
pizza style: New York
> The cracker crisp crust is the highlight at this bright red, order-at-the-counter spot.

Rome's Pizza
300 W. Bitters Rd., 210-490-0700
(+1 other location)
www.romespizza.com
pizza style: thin crust
> It's a case of exotic, eclectic, terrific pizza in a strip mall. Try the "Med-Greek" with gyro meat or the "Taj Mahal" with garbanzos and jalapeños.

Utah

PROVO
Brick Oven Restaurant
111 E. 800 N., 801-374-8800
pizza style: thin crust
> It may look generic, but this place is a BYU tradition, and the thin pizzas and homemade root beer are stellar.

SALT LAKE CITY
Pie Pizzeria
1320 E. 200 S., 801-582-0195
www.thepie.com
pizza style: medium crust
> Graffiti-scrawled college dive with all the prerequisites: good jukebox, plenty of beer, and reliable hand-tossed pizza.

Rusted Sun Pizzeria
2010 S. State St., 801-483-2120
pizza style: New York
> Owner, Wally Stephens, starts with NY-style pizza, then experiments with combos (pineapple and jalapeño) that would make a true-blue Queens pizza man groan. But it's all good.

Stoneground
249 E. 400 S., 801-364-1368
pizza style: New York
> A modern trattoria with pool tables and hip dishes, such as forest-mushroom pizza with goat cheese. All-you-can-eat pizza and salad for $9.95 on Sunday.

Wasatch Pizza Company
820 E. 420 S., 801-359-2300
(+4 other locations)
www.wasatchpizza.com
pizza style: gourmet
> Esoteric takeout/delivery group that offers distinctive, garlicky pizzas such as "The Baja," a mix of shrimp, mushrooms, and roasted garlic on Alfredo sauce.

Wild Mushroom Pizza
2711 S. State St., 801-484-6100
(+1 other location)
www.wildmushroompizza.com
pizza style: gourmet
> Baby pink shrimp? Shiitakes? Spanish pine nuts? Vegan crust and sauce? This isn't your usual takeout/delivery joint.

Vermont

CHARLOTTE
Pizza On Earth
1510 Hinesburg Rd., 802-425-2152
www.pizzaonearth.net
pizza style: thin crust
> In 1992, a former New York technician bought an organic farm, built a wood-fired oven in a tool shed, and started making incredible pizzas topped with recently farmed veggies. Open on Tuesday and Friday.

LUDLOW
Wicked Good Pizza
117 Main St., 802-228-4131
www.wickedgoodpizza.com
pizza style: New York
> In an old house in the Green Mountains, a friendly husband and wife (who live upstairs) oversee the 5 ovens that bake pizzas with 3 different flours in the crust.

PLAINFIELD
Positive Pie
69 Main St., 802-454-0133
pizza style: thin crust
> This spot takes "daily siestas" from 2–4 p.m. It also turns out flatbread pizzas (with toppings as far-flung as felafel and tofu) that were named best in the state by *Vermont* magazine.

STOWE
Pie-casso
Rt. 108 Mountain Rd. 1880, 802-253-4411
www.piecasso.com
pizza style: New York
> Owner Ed Rovetto grew up in his parents' pizzeria, then moved to Stowe to snowboard. Off the slopes, Pie-casso hand-tosses 600 thin-crust pizzas a weekend.

WAITSFIELD
American Flatbread
46 Lareau Rd., 802-496-8856
(+1 other location)
www.americanflatbread.com
pizza style: thin crust
> This "experiment in postmodern baking" attached to a bucolic farm inn morphs from bakery into flatbread pizzeria on Friday and Saturday nights.

Virginia

ALEXANDRIA
Generous George's
3006 Duke St., 703-370-4303
www.generousgeorges.com
pizza style: thick crust
> Between George's floor-to-ceiling '50s kitsch and its chewy, yeasty crusts holding epic portions of specialty toppings, it's a kid-friendly, party-hearty place.

CROZET
Crozet Pizza
5794 Three Notched Rd., 434-823-2132
pizza style: medium crust
> Burlap-covered walls, 8 tables, and one guy making hand-tossed pizza. Wheat or white flour crust, red or white sauce, 35 toppings.

McLEAN
Luciano's Restaurant & Pizzeria
1961 Chain Bridge Rd., 703-893-8488
pizza style: New York
> Cavelike spot in Tyson's Corner mall. The "twice baked" takeout slices are the way to go.

NORFOLK
Cafe Rosso
123 W. 21st St., 757-627-2078
pizza style: thin crust

Executive chef Ben Foote says the wood-burning oven—imported from Italy—makes the real difference at this upscale 21-themed spot. (That's the number of pastas, pizzas, and wines.)

Fellini's
3910 Colley Ave., 757-625-3000
pizza style: gourmet
Some unexpected chic punctuates this Euro-style room where enormous thin pies sport upscale ingredients.

Orapax Inn
1300 Redgate Ave., 757-627-8041
pizza style: medium crust
The homey Greek feel makes it a family favorite. So do the spinach pizzas and the secret Greek spice blend used in the sauce.

RICHMOND
Apollo Restaurant
9410 W. Broad St., 804-965-5554
(+2 other locations)
pizza style: medium crust
This strip-mall spot subscribes to an ambiance-free doctrine for its flame-baked pizzas, which—from white to stuffed to Sicilian—have a loyal following.

Bottoms Up
1700 Dock St., 804-644-4400
(+1 other location)
www.bottomsuppizza.com
pizza style: thick crust
This old building outlived its tobacco warehouse days to become a local pizza tradition. Two outdoor decks overlook train trestles.

Jo-Jo's Pizza
1201 E. Main St., 804-225-9600
www.jojosfamouspizza.com
pizza style: New York slices
Jo-Jo's slices consistently receive the ultimate pizza compliment from dyed-in-the-wool New Yorkers: They have the right amount of everything.

Mary Angela's Italian Subs
3345 W. Cary St., 804-353-2333
pizza style: New York
Locals vie for Mary Angela's pizzas: an ideal balance between crust (slim, not too thin), cheese (melts, doesn't overwhelm), and sauce.

SPRINGFIELD
Delia's Family Restaurant & Pizzeria
6715 Backlick Rd., 703-451-0242
pizza style: New York
The charming owner, Soula Theodorou, says she makes the dough from a secret recipe that involves Coca-Cola and that it's "very tasty and mostly crunchy."

Washington

LANGLEY
Village Pizzeria
108 First St., 360-221-3363
pizza style: New York, New Haven
The New York-born owner, Paul Sarkis, says he learned his craft at PU (Pizza University) on the streets of Brooklyn. Now, on Whidbey Island overlooking Puget Sound, he turns out white clam pies and more.

SEATTLE
Belltown Pizza
2422 First Ave., 206-441-2653
www.belltownpizza.net
pizza style: New York
Everything in this modern spot—from the overhead lights to the glass-topped bar—is red. Except for the pesto sauce on the Northwest pizza (prosciutto, tomatoes, and onions).

A New York Pizza Place
8310 5th Ave. NE, 206-524-1355
www.anewyorkpizzaplace.com
pizza style: New York
Beloved neighborhood joint full of displaced East Coast diehards eating a meat-heavy concoction called "The Godfather."

Pagliacci Pizza
4529 University Way, 206-726-1717
(+5 other locations and 14 delivery kitchens)
www.pagliacci.com
pizza style: Neapolitan
Besides cool combos like goat cheese and prosciutto, Pagliacci offers a seasonal pizza-of-the-month.

Pazzo's Restaurant & Bar
2307 Eastlake Ave. E., 206-329-6558
pizza style: gourmet
The place is all wood and brick, but the pizzas are much fancier. Like the pesto-based "Prada" or the "Bianco," accessorized with chicken and Gorgonzola.

Zeek's
6000 Phinney Ave. N., 206-285-8646
(+5 other locations)
www.zeekspizza.com
pizza style: medium crust
Located in an 80-year-old building downtown, Zeek's has traditional pies, but also serves a hand-tossed Thai veggie pie with homemade peanut sauce.

Washington, D.C.
Alberto's
2010 P St. NW, 202-986-2121
pizza style: thin crust
Alberto's, in a basement with no seating, serves up a great thin crust. And at 2 a.m., after a pub crawl, it's *the* place for a hot slice of cheese.

Pizzeria Paradiso
Dupont Circle 2029 P St. NW, 202-223-1245
pizza style: Italian gourmet
Paradise can be found on the second floor of a row house on Dupont Circle while eating the "Bottarga" pizza bursting with tuna roe.

2 Amys
3715 Macomb St. NW, 202-885-5700
pizza style: Neapolitan
The only D.O.C. pizza in D.C. (That means authentic Neapolitan-style pizza sanctioned by the Verace Pizza Napoletana Association founded in Naples, Italy.)

West Virginia
BECKLEY
King Tut's Pizza Drive-In
301 N. Eisenhower Dr., 304-252-6353
pizza style: thin crust
Classic '50s drive-in with a huge neon sign and metal canopy. Waitresses deliver good all-American fare and rich-sauced pizzas to your car.

Photograph: Kim Rutherford, Courtesy of A New York Pizza Place

DAVIS
Sirianni's Cafe
Route 32/William Ave., 304-259-5454
pizza style: thin crust

On the main drag in a small mountain town, you can smell the garlic coming from Sirianni's, always packed with a diverse crowd.

HUNTINGTON
Monty's Original Pizza
815 Sixth Ave., 304-525-1251
(+7 other area locations)
pizza style: medium crust

Famous for its square slices, Monty's is a downtown tradition. Nice fireplace and framed Elvis pictures.

KANAWHA
The Riverside Anchor
3315 Kanawha Blvd. E., 304-925-9902
pizza style: medium crust

A generous brushing of garlic butter seems to be the key to the "Tomato Pie." Boaters on the Kanawha River can dock, climb a ladder the owner installed, and chow down.

KENOVA
Evaroni's Pizza
914 Oak St., 304-453-4355
pizza style: thin crust

Pickles? On a pizza? Only at Evaroni's, Kenova's community hub. The crispy crust and sweet sauce haven't changed since 1968.

ST. ALBANS
Lorobi's Pizza
2412 Maccorkle Ave., 304-727-4205
pizza style: thin crust

Locals consider Larobi's crackery pizza the ambrosia of the gods, especially "The Big O," a meat and vegetable blast cooked by "little old ladies" in the kitchen.

WHEELING
Dicarlo's Pizza Shop
2099 National Rd, 304-242-1490
(+6 other locations)
www.dicarlospizza.com
pizza style: thin crust

Primo Di Carlo discovered pizza while stationed overseas during WWII. He returned, created his own square "poor man's cheesecake," and sold it for 10¢ a slice. Prices have changed; quality hasn't.

Wisconsin

GREEN BAY
Jake's Pizza
1149 Main St., 920-432-8012
pizza style: medium crust

Owned by a Nordic Packers fan and situated across the street from a punk rock club, Jake's is one of a kind. So are the paper-thin shaved mushrooms on the pizza.

HALES CORNERS
Ann's Italian Restaurant
5969 S. 108th Pl., 414-425-5040
pizza style: thin crust

This converted old house has a lock on Italian comfort food, but the crispy-crusted pizza is the biggest draw.

LA CROSSE
South Lanes Pizza
4107 Mormon Coulee Rd., 608-788-1303
pizza style: thin crust

Not only is this parlor in a bowling alley, the wood tables are made out of the original lanes. The pizzas are old-fashioned, too: no skimping on quality ingredients.

MADISON
Paisan's
80 University Sq., 608-257-3832
www.paisansrestaurant.biz
pizza style: thin crust

This '60s-vintage campus magnet is dark and woody. Live dangerously and ask for the spicy cheese.

MILWAUKEE
Balistreri's Italian-American Ristorante
812 N. 68th St., 414-475-1414
(+1 other location)
www.balistreris.com
pizza style: thin crust

Crammed with Italian clutter and Christmas lights, family-friendly Balistreri's swears by high-butterfat, medium stringy cheese, and canned mushrooms for its unique-tasting pizzas.

Palermo Villa Restaurant
2315 N. Murray Ave., 414-278-7460
pizza style: medium crust

Some say this friendly stalwart reminds them of Tuscany; others insist it's like a small Italian cafe in New York.

Pizza Man
1800 E. North Ave., 414-272-1745
pizza style: thin crust

Barn-board walls and a bell-bottomed logo guy are oh-so '70s. But a subliminal sourdough crust flavor, a lush layer of cheese, zingy toppings (like conch and crab meat), and hundreds of wines by the glass never go out of style.

Zaffiro's
1724 N. Farwell Ave., 414-289-8776
pizza style: thin crust

This modest tavern with Dino on the air-waves and red-checked tablecloths has legions of followers for its pies topped with tangy sauce and flavor-packed sausage.

PEPIN
Harbor View Cafe
314 1st St., 715-442-3893
pizza style: thin crust

Owners Ted and Robbie Fisher grow the vegetables for toppings, the wheat for crust, and raise pigs for sausage—all in the same town as the Laura Ingalls Wilder Museum. (Closed Thanksgiving week through mid-March.)

RACINE
Wells Brothers Italian Restaurant
2148 Mead St., 262-632-4408
pizza style: thin crust

In business since 1921, this is the oldest family-run restaurant in Racine. Wells' enthusiasts have been known to drive in from Iowa just for pizza.

SHEBOYGAN
Il Ritrovo
515 S. 8th St., 920-803-7516
pizza style: Neapolitan

Here the Italian-born owner, Stefano Viglietti, imports everything—including the flour—from the old country.

Nonna Maria
1402 S 8th St., 920-458-3412
pizza style: thin crust

Owner Mary Jo Beniger spent years growing herbs. Now her spice blends add pizzazz to gutsy combos like green cheese and ham and BLT pizzas.

Wyoming

CHEYENNE

L'Osteria Mondello Italian
1507 Stillwater Ave., 307-778-6068
pizza style: Sicilian

Guiseppe Mondello, a native Sicilian, makes a killer white pizza. The airmen of Warren Air Force Base come in droves.

Parkway Pizza
3751 E. Lincolnway, 307-778-2949
pizza style: New York

From its hole-in-the-wall digs to its hand-tossed white pizza, Parkway is a slice of New York in Wyoming.

Pete's Pizza
3229 E. Pershing Blvd., 307-632-2267
pizza style: thin crust

Pete doesn't own the joint anymore, but everything is being done according to his original plan. Current owner Justin Hanker bakes the cheese to a tad overdone, "so that it's a little crispy—like the crust."

JACKSON HOLE

Mountain High Pizza Pie
120 W. Broadway, 307-733-3646
pizza style: medium crust

Jackson Hole is more than a mile high, and the dough at this Western-style parlor has less yeast than more grounded places. But it's wonderfully chewy.

LARAMIE

Grand Avenue Pizza
301 E. Grand Ave., 307-721-2909
(+1 other location)
pizza style: gourmet

There's something charming about eating designer pizza in a pizza parlor hidden away in the Conor Hotel—a historic downtown building

CHAINS

Aurelio's Pizza
708-798-8050
www.aureliospizza.com
Headquarters: Homewood, Illinois
Stores: 41 in 7 states

What started as a suburban storefront in 1959 has grown slowly. Mama Aurelio's thin-crust variety sports a puffy rim, and if you get to the original in Homewood, make like a local and ask for your pie to be baked in the "old oven."

Bertucci's Brick Oven Ristorante
508-351-2500
www.bertuccis.com
Headquarters: Northborough, Massachusetts
Stores: 89 in 14 states

Brought brick-oven pizzas to the masses in the Northeast with its spacious, Tuscan-style restaurants.

California Pizza Kitchen
800-919-3227
www.cpk.com
Headquarters: Los Angeles, California
Stores: more than 150 full-service and 24 ASAP locations in 27 states (and 5 countries)

In the mid-80s, 2 lawyers—standing on the shoulders of Wolfgang Puck and Ed LaDou—quit their jobs to concentrate on hearth-baked gourmet pizzas. A zillion BBQ chicken pizzas later, CPK is a household acronym.

Cassano's Pizza King
937-294-8400
www.cassanos.com
Headquarters: Kettering, Ohio
Stores: 34 in Ohio

A privately owned family company that excels in "Dayton-style" pizza: round pies cut into bite-sized squares with toppings all the way to the edge.

Chuck E. Cheese's
972-258-8507
www.chuckecheese.com
Headquarters: Irving, Texas
Stores: more than 330 in the U.S. and Canada

This pizzeria/entertainment center is kid-heaven: video games, endless drink refills, and live stage shows starring friendly animals.

Cici's Pizza
972-745-4200
www.cicispizza.com
Headquarters: Coppell, Texas
Stores: more than 480 in 26 states

Family-oriented all-you-can-eat buffet concept that has swept across suburbs and small towns in the southeast.

Domino's Pizza
734-930-3030
www.dominospizza.com
Headquarters: Ann Arbor, Michigan
Stores: more than 7,500 worldwide

Ubiquitous Michigan-born pizza empire known for quick delivery and bargain-friendly prices.

Donatos
614-416-7700
www.donatospizza.com
Headquarters: Columbus, Ohio
Stores: 181 in 7 states

In 1963 Jim Grote bet the $1,300 in his pocket on himself and his dream. He went on to build a mega business based on goodwill and trust. Throw in a layer of provolone and edge-to-edge toppings, and you've got a winner.

DoubleDave's Pizzaworks
513-328-3283
www.doubledaves.com
Headquarters: Austin, Texas
Stores: 48 in Texas and 1 in Oklahoma

As popular as DoubleDave's made-to-order pizzas are, their Peproni Rolls (pizza crust rolled around pepperoni and provolone) have become the company's signature product.

Figaro's
888-344-2767
www.figaros.com
Headquarters: Salem, Oregon
Stores: almost 100 in 21 states

Stalwart "we-bake-or-you-bake" company that offers a host of sauces from traditional to spicy picante.

Giordano's
312-641-6500
www.giordanos.com
Headquarters: Chicago, Illinois
Stores: 39, mostly in Illinois

The brothers who started Giordano's had to cut down the amount of garlic they used as it was too much for most mortals. But they didn't back away from their *raison d'être*: stuffed pizza, which they'll ship anywhere in the United States.

Godfather's Pizza
402-391-1452
www.godfathers.com
Headquarters: Omaha, Nebraska
Stores: about 570 in 40 states
Straightforward, kid-friendly 32-year-old pizza chain. Has mercifully toned down the shameless Mafia theme over the years.

Grotto Pizza
302-227-3567
www.grottopizza.com
Headquarters: Rehoboth Beach, Delaware
Stores: 19, mostly in Delaware
On his first day in business in 1960, Dominick Pulieri sold exactly 2 whole pizzas for $1.60 each. Back then, no one in Rehoboth knew what pizza was—but they sure do now.

Happy Joe's Pizza and Ice Cream Parlor
563-332-8811
www.happyjoes.com
Headquarters: Bettendorf, Iowa
Stores: 61 in 6 states
Family-friendly restaurant in the Upper Midwest started by a former North Dakota farmer. Kids love the non-traditional ingredients such as sauerkraut and nacho cheese, and 6 different kinds of Mexican pizzas.

Hungry Howie's
248-414-3300
www.hungryhowies.com
Headquarters: Madison Heights, Michigan
Stores: more than 500 in 18 states
Savvy delivery/takeout operation specializing in flavored crusts.

LaRosa's
513-347-5660
www.larosas.com
Headquarters: Cincinnati, Ohio
Stores: 56 in 3 states
A 50-year tradition that started at a local church festival in Cincinnati's Little Italy. Eat in or invite everyone to your house and order a pizza kit paisano pack with enough stuff to make 6 pies.

Ledo Pizza
410-721-6887
www.ledopizza.com
Headquarters: Annapolis, Maryland
Stores: 71 in 9 states
Its motto—"We are square because we don't cut corners"—is taken literally. The rectangular pizzas are cut into squares, and any dough not used within 2 hours is disposed of and a fresh batch is immediately mixed.

Little Caesars
1-800-7-Caesar
www.littlecaesars.com
Headquarters: Detroit, Michigan
Stores: more than 3,000 nationwide
The fourth member of America's "Big 4" pizza chains was founded—and is still run by—the Ilitch family, owners of the Detroit Red Wings and Tigers. Its innovations since 1959 include drive-through windows and quickie lunch deals.

The Loop Pizza Grill
904-268-2609
www.looppizzagrill.com
Headquarters: Jacksonville, Florida
Stores: 21 in 4 states
Small but steady Southern chain known for its mosaic tile floors and deep-dish pizza. Run by a husband-and-wife team, Mike and Terry Schneider, who named the place for Chicago's downtown area.

Mellow Mushroom
404-505-2801
www.mellowmushroom.com
Headquarters: Atlanta, Georgia
Stores: 71 in 12 states
Started in the 1970s by 2 Georgia Tech roommates, this cartoonish chain now covers the South, mixes its dough with spring water, and remains dedicated to using topnotch ingredients for healthful pizzas.

Monical's Pizza
815-937-1890
www.monicals.com
Headquarters: Bradley, Illinois
Stores: 58 in 3 states
Small chain known since 1959 for its family-friendly outlook (see the "Family Pleaser" meal) and thin, affordable pizzas.

Nancy's Pizzeria
708-444-4411
www.nancyspizza.com
Headquarters: Tinley Park, Illinois
Stores: 42 in 5 states
This ever-expanding stuffed-pizza chain, which made its bones in the Chicago area, oozes with Windy City history.

Noble Roman's Pizza
1-800-585-0669
www.nobleromans.com
Headquarters: Indianapolis, Indiana
Stores: more than 1,250 nationwide and internationally
32-year-old group of quick-service restaurants, many of which are located in malls.

Papa Ginos
1-800-PAPA-GINO
www.papaginos.com
Headquarters: Dedham, Massachusetts
Stores: 180 in 5 states
Founded in Boston in the '60s by a pair of Italian immigrants, this thin-crust chain has spread across New England and now pops up at sports venues and school cafeterias.

Papa John's
502-261-7272
www.papajohns.com
Headquarters: Louisville, Kentucky
Stores: nearly 3,000 nationwide
John Schnatter started by selling pizzas to customers from a broom closet in his father's Indiana tavern in 1984. Now he's the CEO of Papa John's International.

Papa Murphy's
800-257-7272
www.papamurphys.com
Headquarters: Vancouver, Washington
Stores: more than 800
The world's largest take-and-bake chain offers traditional and specialty pies to cook at home for anyone who's sick of delivered pizza arriving cold.

Pizza Hut
972-338-7700
www.pizzahut.com
Headquarters: Dallas, Texas
Stores: nearly 12,000 in 88 countries

From humble beginnings in Kansas in 1958, the red-roofed spot has grown into the most familiar pizzeria the world over. And the biggest: It's continually expanding, now operates from El Salvador to New Zealand.

Pizza King/Sir Pizza
765-289-3321
www.pizzakingindiana.com
Headquarters: Muncie, Indiana
Stores: more than 300 worldwide
What began as Pizza King in Indiana spun off into independently owned Sir Pizza in Tennessee and elsewhere. Trademarks include computerized state-of-the-art conveyor ovens and delivery "as fast as the law allows."

Pizza Schmizza
503-640-2328
www.schmizza.com
Headquarters: Hillsboro, Oregon
Stores: 32 in 2 states
In a dozen years, this chain has extended its reach outside of Oregon to Washington and has its eye on Texas, Utah, California, and Idaho. Are all of those states ready to dig into ostrich-, boar- and alligator-topped pizzas?

Pizzeria Uno
617-323-9200
www.unos.com
Headquarters: Boston, Massachusetts
Stores: 206 worldwide
A mythical old building on the near north side of Chicago—the 1943 birthplace of deep-dish pizza—spawned ubiquitous lesser Uno Chicago Grills (also proffering steaks and seafood) when it franchised in 1979.

Round Table Pizza
925-969-3900
www.roundtablepizza.com
Headquarters: Concord, California
Stores: more than 500 in 8 states
The King Arthur-themed Round Table is one of the largest pizza franchises in the West. 3 generations of California kids have grown up on "Montague's All Meat Marvel."

Sbarro
800-456-4837
www.sbarro.com
Headquarters: Melville, New York

Stores: almost 1,000 nationwide
What began as an Italian grocery store in Brooklyn, circa 1959, has become the largest shopping mall–based restaurant chain in the world. You can even get a slice at the Pentagon.

Shakey's
626-576-0737
www.shakeys.com
Headquarters: Alhambra, California
Stores: 63 in 7 states
50-year-old So Cal-based operation famous for kid-approved thin-crust pizza. Nowhere near its 1970s heyday—but it's huge in the Philippines.

Snappy Tomato
888-463-SNAP
www.snappytomato.com
Headquarters: Florence, Kentucky
Stores: 60 in 6 states
Southern chain known for big buffets, a 6-lb. pizza called "The Beast," and "Snappy," a cutesy tomato mascot.

Valentino's
402-434-9350
www.valentinos.com
Headquarters: Lincoln, Nebraska
Stores: 58 in 6 states
Valentino's fans cheer for the tender, pie-like crust and sauce so thick it needs to be spread on with a spoon. 40 restaurants plus 18 to-go locations make the Valentino's experience mega-accessible to heartlanders.

Vocelli's Pizza
412-279-9100
www.vocellipizza.com
Headquarters: Pittsburgh, Pennsylvania
Stores: 110 in 6 states
This fast-growing company insists on hand-tossed pies and market-fresh toppings in every one of its outlets—the bulk of which are in Pennsylvania.

UNCONDITIONAL LOVE

While writing this book, we got thousands of heartfelt recommendations for people's favorite pizzerias. This one, a plea from Anne-Marie Guarnieri, 30, for Sunrise Inn in Warren, Ohio, was our favorite.

"People who don't like Sunrise Inn pizza are suspect. Be it mentally or socially, there's something not quite right about them. In my family, whether someone liked Sunrise was a good barometer of whether that person was to be liked. From out-of-the-oven hot, to been-sitting-on-the-counter-for-a-while lukewarm, to hey-who-forgot-to-put-this-in-the-fridge room temp, to breakfast-of-champions cold, it's always consistently good. I'm just a simple farmer's daughter from Ohio, but I do know one thing: Life is complicated—pizza shouldn't be. You can have your goat cheese, your saltimbocca, your PINEAPPLE (my GOD!). Give me simple, honest pizza made with love, in a building that may or may not have housed mobsters at one time in history, maybe. Give me Sunrise!"

SELECTED RESOURCES

BOOKS

Buonassisi, Rosario. *Pizza: From Its Italian Origins to the Modern Table.* Richmond Hill, Ontario, Canada: Firefly Books Ltd., 2000.

Deangelis, Dominick A. *The Art of Pizza Making: Trade Secrets and Recipes.* Plains, Pennsylvania: Creative Pizza Company, 1991.

Johns, Pamela Sheldon. *Pizza Napoletana!* Berkeley, California: Ten Speed Press, 1999.

Levine, Ed. *Pizza: A Slice of Heaven.* New York: Universe Publishing, 2005.

Mariani, John: *The Dictionary of Italian Food and Drink.* New York: Broadway, 1998.

McNair, James. *New Pizza.* San Francisco: Chronicle Books, 2000.

Reinhart, Peter. *American Pie: My Search for the Perfect Pizza.* Berkeley, California: Ten Speed Press, 2003.

Scicolone, Charles and Michele. *Pizza: Any Way You Slice It.* New York: Broadway, 1999.

Steingarten, Jeffrey. *It Must Have Been Something I Ate.* New York: Vintage, 2003.

MAGAZINE ARTICLES

Broyles, Tom. "Who is the Father of American Pizza?" *PMQ Magazine,* November/December 2003.

Daniels, Wade. "Wolfgang Puck: Trendsetting Chef Parlays His Name and Fame into an International Brand." *Nation's Restaurant News,* 1/27/03.

Martin, Richard. "California Pizza for the masses; CPK offering Spago-inspired nouvelle pies." *Nation's Restaurant News,* 6/24/85

Pollack, Penny, ed. "Through Thick and Thin." *Chicago* magazine, 7/98.

Ruby, Jeff. "Deep Dissing." *Chicago* magazine, 9/98.

Solomon, Stephen. "Tombstone Pizza Slices Itself a Share of a Growth Market." *Fortune,* 8/28/78.

Spector, Amy. "Ed LaDou: The 'Prince' of Pizza Finds a New Loyal Following." *Nation's Restaurant News,* 3/15/99.

WEB SITES

aboutpizza.com

citysearch.com

correllconcepts.com/Encyclopizza/_home_encyclopizza.htm

geocities.com/Heartland/Flats/5353/pizza

pizzamaking.com

pizzamarketplace.com

pizzatherapy.com

pizzatoday.com

pmq.com

roadfood.com

sliceny.com

verapizzanapoletana.org

PERSONAL INTERVIEWS

Lou Abate, Zachary Allen, Nick Angelis, John Arena, Dan Bacin, Chris Bianco, Steve Brieske, Frank Carney, Tony Consiglio, Steve Coomes, Eileen Cora, Ty Dupuis, Sam Facchini, Efisio Farris, David Grotto, Tony Gemignani, Roger Jehan, Ed LaDou, J.P. LaRussa, Marc Malnati, Jeffrey Moogk, Wolfgang Puck, Rick Rosenfield, Francis Rosselli, George Saxe, Aaron Siegel, Art Smith, Michael Weinstein

Everybody Loves Ice Cream
The Whole Scoop on America's Favorite Treat

By Shannon Jackson Arnold

Paperback $19.99   ISBN: 1-57860-165-7

Three scoops please: a travel book, a cookbook, and a pop culture history all in one, the most complete treatment of the subject a reader can find anywhere. Whether you're looking for a great ice-cream stand nearby, a recipe for rocky road, or an explanation of what makes an ice cream "super-premium," you'll find it here. It's true that *Everybody Loves Ice Cream,* and this book tells you why.

Packed with photos and designed with mix-ins and toppings of all sorts, this charming book is like a trip to the soda fountain—something everybody enjoys. Author Shannon Jackson Arnold covers everything from a factory tour to homemade recipes, from definitions for various frozen desserts to soda jerk jargon.

Everybody Loves Ice Cream provides readers with a look at every aspect of our favorite frozen treat:
- What's the best and where to get it, across the country
- How to make delicious ice cream yourself
- How the manufacturers make it
- Where and how it was invented and how it has evolved
- How it has played a part in American culture

Step right up for a taste of the sweetest book ever!

SHANNON JACKSON ARNOLD is a freelance writer and editor living in Milwaukee, Wisconsin. Her work appears in many magazines, including *Marie Clare* and *Wisconsin Trails,* and she is the former editor of *Ohio* magazine.

To order call: 1(800) 343-4499
www.emmisbooks.com